THE SHARED HEART

PORTRAITS AND STORIES CELEBRATING LESBIAN, GAY, AND BISEXUAL YOUNG PEOPLE

◖

PHOTOGRAPHS BY

ADAM MASTOON

WILLIAM MORROW AND COMPANY, INC./LOTHROP, LEE & SHEPARD BOOKS/NEW YORK

Copyright © 1997 by Adam Mastoon

It is the policy of William Morrow and Company, Inc., and its imprints and affiliates, recognizing the importance of preserving what has been written, to print the books we publish on acid-free paper, and we exert our best efforts to that end.

Mastoon, Adam.
    The shared heart : portraits and stories celebrating lesbian, gay, and bisexual young people / Adam Mastoon.
        p. cm.
    Includes bibliographical references (p. 83).
    ISBN 0-688-14931-6
    1. Gay youth—Portraits. 2. Gay youth—Biography. 3. Coming out (Sexual orientation). 4. Homosexuality. I. Title.
    HQ75.2.M37   1997
    305.235' 08664—dc21   97-3276
                                                                CIP

Printed in the United States of America

First Edition

1 2 3 4 5 6 7 8 9 10

FOR MY DEAR FAMILY AND FRIENDS

Looking back, I cannot recall a single image or role model that mirrored my experience as a gay young man. Without external reflections to validate my internal experience I felt alienated and alone. I imagined that there was something terribly wrong with me. My sexual orientation became a secret sorrow rather than a celebration of love. If only I'd seen and heard other kids who were experiencing similar feelings, I would have recognized myself as part of the world rather than feeling isolated and separate from it. As a gay man and as a photographer, I wanted to make visible the images that I so longed for when I was young.

Growing up is a challenge for everyone. To develop a healthy sense of self, we need reflections that verify and affirm our inner feelings and our external lives. For lesbian, gay, and bisexual young people, these reflections are seldom seen. In school, at home, on television, and in the movies it is difficult to find positive portrayals of the lesbian, gay, or bisexual experience. For these young adults striving to discover their place in the world, the absence of this affirmation can create a dire sense of isolation that is emotionally and spiritually damaging. These young people need and deserve authentic, compassionate images that accurately reflect the humanity and diversity of their lives; images that support their development as young people who possess an integrated sense of themselves and their sexual orientation.

For many lesbian, gay, and bisexual young adults, coming out of isolation and establishing a solid sense of belonging is a frightening process. The fear of being rejected by society, family, and friends can be devastating. Without support and guidance, some young people are so terrified and hopeless that ending their lives feels like the only option. The disturbing fact is that suicide is the leading cause of death among lesbian, gay, and bisexual youth. Now, more than ever, reestablishing a sense of safety and connection for these young people is essential. They must be nurtured and reassured so that they can become healthy, thriving adults.

Thankfully, for many young people, coming out is becoming easier. With support from youth and family organizations, gay/straight alliances in schools, and the availability of lesbian, gay, and bisexual literature, young people are finding positive reflections of themselves that allow them to open to an outer life aligned with their inner feelings.

The Shared Heart brings a human face and a dignified voice to the experiences of lesbian, gay, and bisexual young people. The portraits and stories in this book illuminate the lives of forty exceptional young adults, who dare to be themselves and reveal their deepest challenges and victories. Together they tell a collective story of the courageous journey from silence to expression and from isolation to freedom. They are heroes for our time and role models for us all, embodying honesty and bravery as they stand up and say, "I am who I am and I love who I love." They bring light where there was darkness, and illuminate a pathway through which others can walk.

Meeting and photographing the young people in this book has been a profound experience for me. Their fearless commitment to be themselves deeply inspires me. Their honesty touches the core of our shared human experience and reminds us that deep inside, beyond our differences, we all share the same impulses of the heart.

Open this book. Look into the eyes of these young people. See if you can find the essence of your best friend, your sister or brother, your son or daughter. See if you can find yourself. Look below the surface right to the human being. See the place where we are all the same, and the heart we all share.

THE SHARED HEART

◑

I GREW UP IN A SMALL TOWN JUST OUTSIDE OF BALTIMORE. I REMEMBER BEING TEN YEARS OLD AND THINKING I MUST BE THE ONLY GAY PERSON IN THIS TOWN. I KNEW GAY PEOPLE EXISTED, I JUST THOUGHT THEY LIVED SOMEWHERE ELSE. WHEN I WAS A CHILD, MY ONLY EXPOSURE TO being gay was having the neighborhood children call me "faggot" because I wasn't as "butch" as they were. I was also teased a lot at school.

My family was great, however. They were supportive of all the things I wanted to do, even occasionally playing with my cousin's dolls. My mother insisted that I try the sports thing. I played football in the yard and played in soccer, basketball, and baseball leagues for three years. I enjoyed playing sports, but what I really liked was being with the other boys. All those practices and games with guys that I knew and loved (so I thought) was my way of being gay at that age.

My family never spoke of gay people, not that it was taboo or a bad thing (or a good thing). It just wasn't mentioned. I remember one day my mother, brother, and I were riding home in the car and she said, "We're going to have an important conversation when we get home." My brother and I looked at each other and said, "Oh God, what?" She said, "Sex." (Yuk.) When we got home, she proceeded to tell us about penises and vaginas and how sex is something beautiful between a man and a woman. She said nothing about it being beautiful between a man and another man, or a woman and another woman. I don't blame my mother for not discussing homosexuality, because she was never exposed to it herself.

My brother was very important in the development of my sexuality, although I didn't realize it at the time. He is three years older than I am and he is also gay. He came out to my mother when he went away to college. He and I knew about each other, not because we had discussed it, but because it was understood. We talk about it now and laugh at how we would sometimes look at men on the street and then look at each other and sheepishly smile at our mutual desire and admiration for the male form.

I remained closeted in high school not because I was unsure, but because it was not safe. I knew that when I went to college I could finally be myself. I was waiting for an environment that would be accepting of all differences and not just the difference between varsity and junior varsity.

The safety of college provided me with the freedom to explore and to experience the gay world. In the process I found a great gay and lesbian youth support group. I am now in my third year of college and am the co-president of the group. I am successful and happy, surrounded by the love of all my family and friends, none of whom I lost because of my coming out.

I began to come out to family, friends and anyone I met.
I felt it important to let others know that they knew and loved
a gay person. It's not a sexual thing, It's a human thing.
Love everything and everyone. If you can't, at least accept it,
acknowledge it. Embrace diversity! It's here, it's there its everywhere !!

♡, xoxo
Jamont -20

STEPH

◐

I'M BISEXUAL. BUT I'M ALSO ASIAN AMERICAN. I SAY "BUT" BECAUSE THESE TWO "IDENTI-
TIES" ARE NOT OFTEN VISUALIZED TOGETHER. IN THE UNITED STATES, THE MENTAL IMAGE
THAT PEOPLE HAVE OF A SAME-GENDER-LOVING PERSON IS PREDOMINANTLY WHITE. THE MEN-

tal image that people have of an Asian American is predominantly straight. These are not consciously created mental images, they are subconscious assumptions. For a long time, I thought that I had to pick one or the other. Or that I needed to have a key aspect to define where I "belonged." I tried to figure out what part of me seemed most important.

I got more flak for being Asian American than bisexual, maybe because one can't hide one's race. And while taking flak for something does not neces-sarily make it more important, it does have an effect on one's identity. Going through years of ching-chong-chinaman taunts was terribly unpleasant. Constantly being accused of being a foreigner and told to "go back where (I) came from" was even worse. But being Asian American isn't all negative. Even if given the choice, I wouldn't decide to be white for all the world. I'm proud of my culture, I'm proud of my ethnicity.

It's taken a long time to reconcile my two identi-ties. There were other things that my classmates made fun of as well. They teased me about my young age, I graduated from high school when I was fifteen, and about being a science-oriented female, which in my conservative school was looked upon as an oddity. In the gay, bisexual, lesbian community we are often told we should be able to "be who we are," but when one is many things, all equally important, it is some-times difficult.

Although every individual has his or her own cir-cumstances with which to deal, there are still a wide range of things each of us can do to foster tolerance and acceptance of all sexualities. We can provide comfort to others who are gay, bisexual, lesbian, or questioning. We can educate about our lives, our exis-tences, our rights. We can influence politics, we can create art, we can compile histories, we can provide resources.

I've been working with the gay, bisexual, and les-bian Asian/Pacific community. Collecting histories. Doing outreach. Organizing events. Since one of my hobbies and skills has been writing web pages, I've put much of the information I've accumulated on the Web. Here's the address: (http//www.tufts.edu/~stai/QAPA/resources.html). My hope is that this information can help others realize that there is indeed a community of us out here. My vision is that there will be increased awareness in the gay, bisex-ual, and lesbian communities about people of color, and increased awareness within Asian/Pacific American communities about being gay, bisexual, and lesbian.

For years I have been trying to sort out how I feel about being both Asian American and bisexual. I am a minority within a minority. Growing up, I saw no images of gay Asians or Asian Americans. All the gay, bisexual, and lesbian people I interacted with were white. In the Asian American community, gayness was seen as a "Western problem." There was no one with whom to share my experiences. When I finally met other gay, bisexual, and lesbian people who also shared similar ethnic backgrounds, it was incredible. I realized I didn't need to choose one identity over the other.

—Steph, age 22

DON

◑

IVIDLY REMEMBER THE FIRST TIME I WAS ATTRACTED TO ANOTHER BOY. IT WAS SUNDAY, AUGUST 21, 1988, AND IT WAS MY FRIEND'S TWELFTH BIRTHDAY PARTY. HIS DAD DECIDED TO TAKE A BUNCH OF US TO YANKEE STADIUM TO SEE A BALL GAME. THIS KID, WHOM I'D NEVER seen before, came along with us. I was very attracted to him but I had no idea what those feelings meant or why. One thing for sure was that I felt disgusted that I got turned on by another guy.

When I was sixteen years old, I began to seriously question my sexuality. I really wanted to tell people about the feelings I was having but was afraid of getting hurt physically, emotionally, and mentally. I didn't feel like losing my friends or being called names. I decided to talk to a very close friend. Luckily, he was accepting and said it didn't change anything.

I didn't tell anyone else for a while. Eventually I told this girl in my class who I thought I could trust. She acted very accepting and swore that she wouldn't tell anyone. A few weeks later, I found out that she told several other people because she "didn't know how to handle it." By that time, I was petrified because I didn't know how to react. Should I deny everything and stay in the closet or should I tell the truth and be proud of who I am?

I decided to be honest with everyone, so I told my friends, or people I thought were my friends, that I was gay. They acted very accepting at first, but they gradually stopped calling me to hang out with them. I felt ignored and betrayed. I began to feel like a social outcast. My junior and senior years of high school, which are supposed to be fun, were simply hell. I couldn't wait to get out of there.

I let my father know that I was gay when I was sixteen. Doing this took more guts than just about anything. I never really cared for my father until after I came out to him. I always felt that he never understood me. But if it weren't for his support, I wouldn't be where I am today,

I am going to describe my father. He is six feet, six inches, 230 pounds, and a gym teacher in the Bronx. He isn't exactly the kind of guy you would want to approach and explain to that you are gay. I can remember him making anti-gay comments ever since I was young.

I was so scared to find out my father's reaction. To my pleasant surprise, he told me that I am who I am and that I didn't choose to be gay. He believes that you are born gay. I agree, and also believe that your sexuality is based on your biology, genes, and environment.

My father gave me the inner strength to come out at a young age. A month after I came out to him, just before school started we were sitting on the front steps of my house. I was really scared to enter my junior year of high school. I thought my father would have some advice on whether I should come out in school. He told me that I could never respect myself unless I was proud of who I am and I was able to hold my head up with dignity. He said that I didn't have to go around in school shouting that I was gay, but that I shouldn't lie to my friends. If they couldn't accept me for who I am, they weren't worth it. That single talk with my father inspired me to come out of the closet and get it over with. Looking back, I'm glad I came out—I had to go through hardships, but it made me a stronger person.

I think a great deal of stress is lifted when you come out to people because you don't feel like you're deceiving them. I don't feel like I'm hiding anything. I enjoy coming out to people because I look at it as an educational and enlightening experience. Some people act very surprised, because I don't fit their mold of a gay male teenager.

Don
Age: 19

KATIE

◑

THE DAY ADAM CAME TO TAKE OUR PICTURE WAS THE FIRST TIME I EVER REALLY LOOKED INTO MY MOTHER'S EYES AND UNDERSTOOD HER AS SOMEONE MORE THAN MY MOTHER. WE WOKE UP EARLY AND TALKED OVER COFFEE ABOUT WHAT WE SHOULD WEAR. WE COULDN'T match, but we had to be consistent. I laughed at my mother's choice in clothes, something only a daughter can do, and she told me for the millionth time not to worry, that I looked "cute."

For the first time in my life my mom was going to bravely step forward and publicly acknowledge that she is a lesbian. Not that she hadn't before, but she had never done so within this sort of context. And for all of the times I've declared my own sexuality to her, it no longer felt like a separation, but a connection.

Ever since I came out as a lesbian I did everything in my power to separate my identity from my mom's. I was so scared that people would think that she was a bad mother, that I didn't want to acknowledge our similarities. I also wanted to experience the gay culture alone. Yet at the same time I needed her support. It was a constant push-pull of emotion as I slowly became more comfortable with both of our identities.

When Adam arrived, we had no idea what to expect. He explained what the morning would be like, and after signing papers my mom said she would leave me and Adam alone, something she is used to doing when I have friends over. Only this time, she was supposed to stay. We tromped outside into the overcast day, and stood in my buggy backyard while the camera was set up. Then it was time to pose. While it hadn't been long since we last hugged, my mother and I awkwardly put our arms around each other for what felt like the first time. It was a beginning, a renewal. It felt like the first time that we had embraced one another as individuals, connected by blood and integrated by the fact that we are both gay.

We were very quiet as the first few pictures were taken, not sure what to say to one another. When we normally talk there is a time constraint—she has to go to work, or I have to go out with friends. We don't always sit down and talk for no reason. Slowly I began making funny little comments, beginning to act as I do around my friends. I was trying to relax, loosen up, and pretend that every day I have a camera in my face. My mom began to relax too, and our arms sort of melted into a hug. When we changed positions I found myself looking right into my mother's eyes. I saw a part of myself there. For the first time I felt that I understood who she was. She was not just a mother, but a social worker, a lover, a daughter, a lesbian. In our hug, we entwined a ring of protection around ourselves. We both know the pain and isolation of homophobia, and have shed similar tears because of it. In our hug, I felt strong and powerful, and able to take on the world. Never in my life have I felt the kind of support we gave to each other then, and continue to give one another now.

We have entered a new stage of our relationship, what I would like to consider an adult stage. While neither of us cares to share all the intimate details about my girlfriend or her partner, we help each other enjoy our days together. Even if it is eating a bowl of cereal together, my mom and I trust this new adventure. We tolerate more, enjoy more, and fight less. I have realized how strong my mother is, and understand how many battles she has fought in her life. I also realize how lucky I am to have her support and friendship. We are two generations coming together and facing the world, a task that is not easy to do. And although there will always be the constant mother/daughter push and pull about the telephone, who walks the dog, and my curfew, our connection as mother and daughter will always remain strong.

My family is not a "typical" family. We are not all related by blood, but we are still a family. I have four "parents" and two homes. My biological mother is a lesbian and lives with her partner in one of my homes. We have four cats and a dog and enjoy the connection we share as lesbians. We make gay jokes together, and share our lives just as any other family. My dad and his partner live together at my other home. They are both very supportive of me and have been throughout my coming out process. I also have an older brother who I adore. He is twenty and lives at college. We talk on the phone and complain about women and our parents. I love my family, complications and all. Family is not always biological, sometimes you have to create it on your own. Family is what you make it. Katie, 17 ☺

ALTON

◑

ON MY WAY TO SCHOOL, THERE IS THIS ONE BEND IN THE ROAD RIGHT BEFORE WE GET ON THE HIGHWAY. EVERY MORNING, HALFWAY THROUGH THE TURN, THIS SICKENING SENSE OF NAUSEA GRUMBLES IN MY GUT. AS WE GET CLOSER, MY WHOLE BODY SLOWLY GOES NUMB.

I can feel it. I guess I'm turning part of myself off. I can feel the cold sensation move from my shoulders down to my toes. By the time I get to the door, part of me isn't there, and I'm just numb. This is how I go to school.

Before, the nondescript faces used to drop gay slurs, but now they look away as I pass. When I sit down others get up, or get this uncomfortable look on their faces and their eyes dart around nervously, but no one ever says anything. When I don't have classes I go and hide in offices or the library, just so I don't have to deal with the glances, but the glances never turn into violence. My friends, the headmaster's daughter, and the dean of minority students are comfortable using "fag," "queer," "homo," "gay," as derogatory slurs in public, but they're not directed at me anymore. I tell them that I don't feel safe. "But no one is harassing you," they say. I guess I'm "lucky."

I can remember being confused about my feelings for boys as early as elementary school. I admitted to myself that those feelings were an attraction in sixth grade, but at the time I had never met a gay, lesbian, or bisexual person, and while I had heard the terms used derogatorily all the time, I never knew what they *really* meant. It wasn't until eighth grade that I figured out that being attracted to boys meant I was gay. That realization was so depressing because suddenly all of the gay jokes, "faggot," and "that's so gay" comments I heard so often, applied to me. The sense of "it's not okay to be gay" that seemed to be everywhere was why I was afraid to tell people that I was gay for so long. When I went to high school, I just tried not to think about it, but there came a point where ignoring that part of myself became debilitating. I remember telling myself that I just had to tell someone, just one person. That person was a friend who had gone off to college. We were talking early one morning, at the beginning of my sophomore year, and I said I had something I needed to tell her. I couldn't bring myself to say, "I'm gay," so I made her guess. She did, eventually. It was a great comfort that someone else knew, that I didn't have to keep all of this bottled up inside of me, that I could talk about it. Slowly, I became less afraid about telling people, and over a period of a few months, I began to come out to my friends, teachers, and before my sixteenth birthday, my parents. When I told my parents, I handed each of them a letter I had written and a twenty-page packet of information, asked them to read, and just sat there. They had a lot of questions, but their reaction was simply that they loved me regardless of anything. I don't think it could have gone any better.

Beyond the sense of liberation and freedom that accompanied my coming out, I have also felt a remarkable sense of clarity. Before coming out, I can remember lying awake in bed at night being simultaneously petrified and resigned to never being able to be happy. Questions and fears would fly through my head: — "Will I ever be able to have a family?" or "Everyone will hate me." — While coming out has not been without its dark points, the uncertainty has passed. I am now at a place where I see that I am capable of doing so much. Before I came out, I wasn't sure I would be able to grow up. Now, I am out, have grown up — some, and now nothing can stop me from being happy.

— Alton, 17

JESSICA

◐

NOT A SINGLE PERSON I CAME OUT TO REACTED BADLY. I CAME OUT TO MYSELF WHEN I WAS THIRTEEN. AT FOURTEEN, I TOLD MY BEST FRIEND. SHE SAID SHE HAD KNOWN FOR A LONG TIME AND HAD JUST BEEN WAITING FOR

me to tell her. I came out to more friends after that. But I was afraid that people would think I was disgusting and would stop hanging out with me. It was hard enough trying to be cool in high school without people knowing I was a lesbian.

When I was fifteen, I came out to a girl whom I was becoming friends with. I was sick of lying and I trusted her. She was fine when I told her, but a week later I found out that she had told three of her closest friends and they told their friends and it had pretty much become a big piece of gossip. She didn't do it out of malice; she just couldn't keep her mouth shut. I was horrified and pretended to be sick so I wouldn't have to face anyone at school. My grandparents, whom I lived with then, became suspicious, so I figured it would be a good time to come out to them. I know they were surprised, but they got used to it. I couldn't stay home from school forever, and when I did go back it wasn't as bad as I thought. But I still felt exposed and wondered what people were thinking. Almost no one said anything, but I could tell that they were looking at me differently. I heard that people made the girl who outed me feel pretty awful about what she'd done. One of her friends came up to me and told me not to worry and that I was really lucky to have such good friends. After that I was a little more comfortable and stopped worrying so much about what anyone thought.

When I had been out for a while and the gossip died down, a few other people, who didn't want anyone else to know, came out to me and I was glad to be trusted. I was able to be there for them because I had had support from my family and friends.

I developed confidence and became politically active. When I was sixteen I was appointed to the Massachusetts Governor's Commission on Gay and Lesbian Youth. The commission was created to address the high suicide rate among gay and lesbian teenagers. I ended up doing a lot of public speaking about my experience for the commission. Many of my friends' parents would have been horrified if their kids had been as visible as I was, but my grandparents understood the importance of my activism. I never imagined that I'd ever be so out. I was lucky to be able to take something that was so scary at first and turn it around.

Now that I have a girlfriend, that brings up different issues. Being part of a couple makes me feel as though I have to come out all over again. Can I tell people about her? What if I want to bring my girlfriend to family gatherings? Will they be uncomfortable? Will they pretend she's just another friend? When we're in public, can we hold hands? Can I give her a kiss? It's frustrating to worry about people's reactions. Being part of a couple is forcing me to deal with what it really means that I'm a lesbian—I am in love with a woman. It's not just a label anymore.

I've been out for six years and being a lesbian isn't a big deal to me anymore. I can't imagine what it would be like not to be out. I get angry that some people can't have this because they are surrounded by so much homophobia. I don't have any illusions about how safe the rest of the world is, but I can't imagine having to hide who I am on a daily basis. It just seems so ridiculous that anyone would have a problem with people being in love.

Jessica, 20

MATT

◑

MY PARENTS SIGNED ME UP FOR GYMNASTICS CLASSES AT A GYM NEAR MY HOUSE. ONE AFTERNOON ONE OF MY INSTRUCTORS RECOMMENDED THAT I SWITCH TO A MORE LEARNING-INTENSIVE GYM. AT THE AGE OF EIGHT, I WAS FORMALLY INTRODUCED INTO the world of competitive gymnastics and it began to consume a major part of my life. Weekends with friends were often sacrificed for competitions. By the time I was sixteen, I was eating, sleeping, and breathing gymnastics.

It was during this period that my parents were getting divorced, and I was questioning my own sexuality. Gymnastics became a way that I could vent my feelings of anger, sadness, and excitement. The gym became the place where I could get away from everything. It was the one thing in my life (at that time) that I knew I could excel and succeed at.

My mom was the first person to know that I was gay. *She asked me,* I told her yes, and she said that she still loved me just the same and that it was okay to be who I am. A few weeks later she sent me to Miami to visit her cousin who is also gay. I was only fourteen at the time and knew that there was much to learn about the community that would eventually play a major part in my life.

I told my mother that she could tell my father: I didn't think I was quite comfortable enough to talk to him about it myself. He thought it was a phase at first, but after a few weeks he realized that I was not going to change. He introduced me to some friends of his who were gay. It was a great experience to meet adults who could be positive role models for me.

I came out because I was tired of leading a double life. People always assumed that I was straight. (Although I have no idea how on earth they were able to come to this conclusion given the fact that most women have deeper voices than I do.) For me, coming out was a necessity. I was screaming inside for someone to recognize who I was and to say that it was okay.

At the end of my junior year, I made the decision to come out to everybody. And, boy, let me tell you, it only took two days to come out to twelve hundred kids. I began by telling one of my closest friends. By the end of the following day, *everyone* knew. I'd be sitting in the common room studying, and kids would come up to me and ask me questions like "What's it like to be gay?" or "Do you know anyone else who's gay in our school?" By coming out I was able to educate students and faculty members about what it's like to be gay. A week after I came out, a teacher from my school also came out. Almost all of the responses we received were positive. I was extremely fortunate to be in such an accepting atmosphere.

Once I came out and began to feel more comfortable with who I was, I started to realize that gymnastics had consumed a major part of my life. After my freshman year of college, I quit gymnastics and went home to attend a local university.

Now that I'm out and about, I feel free to be myself. There's no need to hide from myself, or pretend to be someone I'm not. Coming out to myself before I came out to anyone else was absolutely essential. Until I recognized who and what I was, life was hell. I didn't have any sense of self-worth. Since discovering the small part of who and what I am, my sense of self-esteem has grown tremendously.

I BEGAN GYMNASTICS WHEN I WAS SIX YEARS OLD AND COMPETED TILL I WAS TWENTY. MY FIRST YEAR AT COLLEGE EVERYONE ON THE TEAM INCLUDING THE COACH KNEW THAT I WAS GAY. IT WAS SO MUCH EASIER TO BE MYSELF AS OPPOSED TO PRETENDING TO BE SOMEONE ELSE. I WAS A LITTLE NERVOUS STARTING AT A NEW SCHOOL, NOT KNOWING ANYONE, AND YET THE ENTIRE TEAM KNOWING ABOUT ME. LUCKILY THERE WERE SOME OTHER KIDS ON THE TEAM WHO I'D COMPETED AGAINST IN PREVIOUS YEARS WHO WERE MY FRIENDS. THEY HELPED ME THROUGH WHEN TIMES WERE ROUGH. OF COURSE THERE WERE THOSE TEAM MEMBERS WHO KNEW THAT I WAS GAY AND WEREN'T OKAY WITH IT. ALTHOUGH THEY WERE NOT ACCEPTING, THEY STILL GAVE ME THE RESPECT THAT I DESERVED.

— Matt, age 22

KERRY

◐

RIGHT NOW, I IDENTIFY MY SEXUAL ORIENTATION AS BEING SOMEWHERE BETWEEN BISEX-UAL AND GAY, BUT WHEN I FIRST CAME OUT IT WAS BISEXUAL. I WAS NAIVE ENOUGH TO THINK THAT BEING BI MEANT THAT I WOULD NEVER BE ABLE TO HAVE A MONOGAMOUS

relationship, or be satisfied being with just one person. It was only through talking with other bisexuals, reading many books, and taking a long time to decide what was right for me that I finally learned that bisexuality meant nothing more than I was attracted to people of either gender. It doesn't mean I have to be attracted to both simultaneously. In fact, I find that my sexuality is very mercurial. Some days, weeks, months, I feel more gay than straight. Other times I feel more straight than gay, and it really doesn't matter.

Superficially, my life is very similar to the lives of my heterosexual peers. I go to school, scramble through my classes, blow through homework, and maybe go out with my friends or down to the coffeehouse for some cheap conversation. I can't say that being gay has made life any easier. It has definitely altered the types of activities that I participate in. Were I not gay, I probably would not have felt compelled to found and run my school's gay/straight alliance. Activism has become almost a default position for me. I wouldn't know what to do if I wasn't planning some workshop or meeting, or running off to a speaking engagement. Being out, I feel responsible to make school safer for those who can't come out.

My gay/straight alliance adviser has been a mentor to me. First of all, the woman has never had a bad hair day. She has fought the administration at my school to protect the rights of the students who attend the GSA, and she has single-handedly prevented the administration from shoving us back into the closet. For the three years I've known her, she has put herself on the line to help other people. My respect for her knows no bounds.

A huge difference has also been made in my life by Governor William Weld. His fearless support of antidiscriminatory legislation has made my high school career much safer than it otherwise would have been. He has created a statewide environment in which it is not only relatively safe to be a gay student, but where gay students are protected, supported, and affirmed. I am amazed at the legal progress made under Weld's jurisdiction. I am grateful to him for being a role model, and for making Massachusetts a positive example to the nation and world in terms of gay civil rights.

Becoming an activist and joining the Massachusetts Student Speaker's Bureau helped me to meet more gay people than anything else I've done. I've also joined some youth groups, and of course, there's my school's gay/straight alliance. I've met a lot of gay people locally since I came out. It's made me a safe person for others to come out to as well. A lot of people feel comfortable being themselves around me because I'm comfortable with myself. It's taken an awfully long time to get this far. It has also taken the support of my family, friends, and teachers, along with my own soul-searching.

I am not out to my extended family, and I hate it. I've left it to my mother's discretion to tell my relatives. I come from a very traditional Italian family, and she will probably bear the brunt of any backlash that may, and probably won't, occur. It makes conversations during holidays a bit awkward. Invariably, my grandparents ask about "that group" I run at school, or what I do with "that student speaker's bureau" and I have to bite my tongue and dance around the issue replacing the term "gay/straight alliance" with "diversity group." Meanwhile, I'm trying not to laugh because my sister is listening to how carefully I'm skirting the fact that I'm gay, and finding the entire situation as ludicrous as I do.

I'm going off to college a year early, and I'll be living in New York City; things should be easier than they were in high school. I might have liked to graduate with my class, but I don't think I would have made it. I probably would have dropped out if I'd had to face another year of high school. The awful thing is that I love school. I love to learn, but for me it wasn't about learning anymore. It was about making it through the day in one piece. Now that I've graduated, high school is beginning to seem like a bad dream, and I'm finally waking up.

Kenny
(age 16)

◖

AT AGE TWELVE I WASN'T YET WILLING TO THINK OF MYSELF AS GAY OR EVEN BISEXUAL, BUT I KNEW THAT I LIKED MEN. AND KEEPING THESE INTENSE, SECRETIVE, AND SUPPOSEDLY FORBIDDEN DESIRES ALL COOPED UP INSIDE BECAME UNBEARABLE. IT WAS TIME

to talk to someone about my feelings. But how? Whom could I trust? The level of risk seemed immeasurable. My solution was fairly creative but still risky. It wasn't until the fall of eighth grade that I began to take action. Ever since my parents got divorced when I was five, my mother always told me that if I ever felt the need to "talk with someone," I could. So I used that as my excuse and searched around my hometown for a psychotherapist. I didn't want just anyone either. I wanted a gay psychotherapist. I called the local gay and lesbian community center, got some referrals, and talked with several therapists over the phone.

That's how I found David. In my first session with him I remember that I didn't share anything of my "big secret." But slowly I began to come out to him. I told him about my desires and fears. But mostly, I asked him lots of questions. I wanted to know if the stereotypes I grew up with were true. I wanted to know what his life was like as an adult gay man. Ultimately, I wanted to find out where I fit in the spectrum of sexuality.

After several weeks of working with David, I began to feel I wanted to find out what was "out there" in the gay community. David suggested I go to the local gay and lesbian youth group, which I decided to do. Going to the Thursday night youth meeting proved, in time, to be an invaluable resource. My sense of self and sexuality blossomed. Most important, I became part of a community. I had a group of friends who understood everything that was

going on. I relied on them a great deal. They gave me the strength to make it through. I never would have been so brave and "out" without my Thursday night friends. We were a crew. We were there for each other through lots of tears and triumphs. We shared stories of being beaten up—in the streets and at school, of our first loves, of being thrown out of the house, of being tested for HIV, of the joy of coming out to a friend who still loved us just the same, of sneaking into local bars, and much more.

Over time, the Thursday night meetings became my main source of support. I continued to have my sessions with David and eventually our work came to an end. David was an inspiration to me. He answered my flood of questions honestly and patiently. He warned me of things to watch out for in the community and shared his own experience with me. He never tried to represent the whole gay community. I never felt David wanted me to be gay, either. He didn't have a personal investment in where I ended up on the sexual spectrum. He just wanted to support me in my search. He left the choices and conclusions up to me. To this day I can't imagine how coming out would have been without him.

As for the Thursday night crew, I still wonder what has become of them. I wonder whether they realize how lucky we were to have each other. We didn't feel lucky at the time. We often felt scared and alone. But I know that for those three years, I prayed for Thursdays to come quickly, knowing that my friends would pull me through.

Being gay for me is equal parts pain and joy. It is a journey of healing the wounds of shame and fear that are created by our society and of celebrating my honest expressions of love. When my pain is most present, I remind myself again and again to expand my capacity to love myself and to be loved by others.

I have come to realize that being gay encompasses much more than my sexuality. It inspires not just who I love but how I love. And not just how I love men, but how I love women, my family and non-gay men. My gayness is mystical. It is rooted in how I create art, play, touch, dance, make love and pray. For me, being gay is a mystical journey and a healing potion.

Chi, 20

CHAYA

◐

S A SMALL CHILD, I KNEW THERE WAS SOME COMPONENT TO MY BEING THAT WAS DIFFER-ENT FROM THAT OF OTHER CHILDREN. IT FELT LIKE A VAGUE ABSENCE FLOATING SOME-WHERE IN MY SUBCONSCIOUS. WHEN MY FRIENDS STARTED TO LIKE GUYS AND GIGGLE

about them I laughed along. When they teased me about liking a particular boy, I insisted that it was not true. They wondered why I insisted so strongly. I wanted them to know the truth, but I could not find the words to express it.

One day in junior high, I had an anxiety attack. It was only years later that I realized that that day was the start of my coming out process. I remember lying curled on my quilt, staring at my lacy curtains feeling truly alone for the first time. It terrified me that there was nothing I could do to make myself feel better. I couldn't get help from my mother or aspirin, or anything else that had given me comfort before. I felt that this was the start of something bigger, and that from now on, my own battles would be fought in single combat. Maybe that realization was what scared me the most. I was to spend years trying to overcome this beast.

Before fifth grade, I was surrounded by friends. I was a cheerful, generous child. Then, without warning, I was suddenly alone. My friends refused to talk to me and regarded me as a horrible creature. My classmates didn't seem to know I was gay, but they knew that a change was taking place. Suddenly, the basis for popularity was no longer general kindness, but some mystery called "fashion" and "cool," which meant being more feminine than I could ever be. For this they gave me no peace. Throughout junior high and high school, I never once walked down the halls without someone yelling some horrible taunt. The teachers would see this going on, or even look me straight in the eye as people yelled at me, and they would walk on by, leaving me to the will of the boys hurling death wishes at me. There was a time when I got a lot of prank calls at home, including death threats, terrifying my dear parents, making me very ashamed.

One time, when I sat with a group of girls at lunch, they stared at me and, one by one, got up and left me

sitting alone with my plate of limp spaghetti. I was always alone. For the next two years, I lived with anxiety attacks as a constant companion. They came at night, when I lay in bed trying to glide into sleep. Most nights I would stay up for hours, aching for morning. I could not eat and began to lose weight. It seemed my body was a physical representation of the mental disintegration that overcame me. After two long years, I had an attack that was so overwhelming that it left me with no words, no way of crying out.

For a year or so, my life was empty. I went through months without much feeling or passion. The attacks became fewer and further apart. The emptiness felt good, as if I was being cleansed of all the old dead debris. I remember a slow aching feeling that I was gay. It seeped into me and became a normal part of my life. It seemed like such an easy thing to accept at the time, because I realized that the dark days before had been the real struggle. Now I understood what I had fought for all that time.

Much to my surprise, high school eventually ended. I put on my cap and gown and suddenly relief overwhelmed me. I would never have to go back there again. I slowly gained back the weight I had lost and learned to love myself.

Coming out made me rethink my priorities in a way I never would have otherwise. Many assumptions crumbled away. I learned how to plan my life around the woman I saw in the mirror and not skim through life assuming I would be happy if I got a nice desk job in an office, had a husband, and somehow learned to be feminine and wear a dress. When I got to know myself, I learned that I am made to live in my boots and flannels, going to high schools and communities around the country with a group of people sharing our life stories as queer people and working for human rights.

I came out because the loneliness of the closet was sucking all of the life out of my body. I did not have a choice. I needed to come out in order to survive, but I was terrified of loosing my beloved family and friends and of facing up to my own homophobia. Then one day, when I was feeling feisty, I gathered all of the courage I could find (even from my eyelids I think) and began to tell my long-kept secret. I felt so relieved that I no longer had to spend my life in hiding, I remember crying to myself.

-Chaya
20 years old

FROM AS FAR AS I CAN REMEMBER, I'VE ALWAYS BEEN GAY. I REMEMBER PLAYING WITH MY AUNT'S WIGS. I REMEMBER MY GRANDMOTHER HELPING ME WHEN I PLAYED DRESS-UP, WHICH ALWAYS SEEMED TO BE IN WOMEN'S CLOTHES. I REMEMBER HAVING MANY MORE

female friends and picking up sassy-girl comebacks and gestures. Adults seemed to like what I was doing and I was just being myself. Even before the age of five I said I wanted to be a girl. Looking back on that makes me laugh, since I really love being a man and would never think of changing my gender. I am a gay man, it's that simple. I can see how I wanted to be a girl when I was a child. I mean, I was attracted to other boys, I wanted to be nurturing, and I wanted to be "pretty" and "cute." I know now that I can be all of those things and still be a man.

As I got older, the name-calling began. From fifth until probably ninth grade, I was always known as the fag. I was not the best in sports and had a high-pitched voice before it changed into the baritone register it is now. I sang in the church choir and was in chorus, and loved acting. I did school plays like there was no tomorrow. I never thought of it as a gay thing, but others did.

I never heard the word "gay" until I was about seven. I remember watching an entertainment program that featured a show called "Brothers" which ran a clip of what they called the "gay character." The man in the clip was flitting around the house wearing a sheer pink scarf tied tightly around his neck. The scarf reminded me of those my aunt had. The audience in the clip was applauding and laughing as the gay character flitted around the house, and I thought "He is cool! Everyone thinks he is so funny . . . that's going to be me."

While I was in Junior high I tried to butch up my image and listen to heavy metal and wear denim and flannel instead of the latest styles. I was gonna be a bad ass. It didn't work. I got tired of trying to be cool and butch. The records never got played since I was always listening to Debbie Gibson's new album, *Electric Youth*. The clothes quickly went to the back of the closet and I became preppy me again.

In high school my hormones kicked in full blast. I remember scoping out the cute guys in the senior class when I was a freshman. I would never tell anyone about my attraction to men. I remember sneaking down to my living room late at night to watch *Torch Song Trilogy* on cable, since it was a story about a gay man. The kiss between Brian Kerwin and Matthew Broderick is one I will never forget. It was the first time I ever saw two men kissing. I videotaped the movie and watched that scene over and over again. It was the most wonderful thing to see—two gorgeous men kissing!

Theatre is probably the thing that inspires me most in my life. I have always loved performing. I am persuing my dream of being an actor and director. When I was younger, I spent my afternoons practicing for the soccer and swim teams. I was not the sports jock that all the other boys I grew up with wanted to be. Theatre is my gift. The arts are where I belong. I can finally express myself totally, through directing and performing. It is the reason I get up in the morning and the reason I go to sleep at night.

— WILL, 20

SHANNY

◐

I AM IN LOVE WITH MY GIRLFRIEND AND HAPPY TO BE IN LOVE WITH ANOTHER WOMAN. IT FEELS GOOD TO CARE FOR SOMEONE DEEPLY AND HAVE THE FEELINGS RECIPROCATED. I DO NOT FEEL I SHOULD KEEP OUR LOVE A SECRET. MY FAMILY AND OTHERS SHOULD LOOK AT WHO I AM AS an individual and not at whom I sleep with. When I came out to my parents and siblings, my mother had the hardest time dealing with the fact that I am bisexual and presently in love with another woman. Recently I proposed to my girlfriend and she accepted. We told my parents and brother, my sisters were not around. My father congratulated us and my mother walked in another direction. My brother did not say anything negative or positive. He said he had to think about it.

My girlfriend and her daughters inspire me each day. I feel very fortunate to have them in my life. It has been great watching the two girls ages five and seven grow and change. My parents also inspire me. They adopted me when I was a year old and brought me to this country from Seoul, Korea. If not for them, I probably would not be alive today. They have a house and about twenty-eight acres of land and work extremely hard. They have been together for twenty-six years. My roommate inspires me every day as well. She has cerebral palsy. I am her personal assistant and part-time case manager. Seeing the challenges she overcomes each day is inspiring.

This is my vision for the future: I hope that coming out is easy for others. I hope that same-sex marriages soon will be legal. I hope that people will see us as individuals rather than whom we are intimate with. I hope that young adults do not get discriminated against because of their sexual orientation.

I do not feel I need to hide my sexual orientation, at the same time I do not flaunt it. I am comfortable with who I am. My "style" is smooth... clean, short haircut, neat dressy attire for a sort of professional respectable appearance. I am pretty easy going and out going.

What's most important for people to know is that I am Shanny, an Amerasian proud bisexual woman. I am not going to change for anyone because I'm me. ACCEPT ME AS I AM !!!

SHANNY
21

ADAM

◑

I READ SOMETHING REALLY FUNNY THE OTHER DAY—THIS GUY, WHO WAS OBVIOUSLY PRETTY HOMOPHOBIC, TALKED ABOUT HOW THE QUEER POPULATION OF AMERICA COULDN'T BE MORE THAN 1 PERCENT BECAUSE HE DIDN'T KNOW MANY HOMOSEXUALS. I LAUGHED WHEN I READ it—obviously, he was enough of a jerk that the gay people he knew didn't bother to come out to him. It's funny that we homosexuals have this power of invisibility. We can pass for straight with such ridiculous ease. People are *presumed* straight until proven otherwise. It can be useful, but, also problematic.

When I came out, I decided despite society's attitudes that there was nothing wrong with me because of my sexuality. Once I honestly felt good about myself and being gay, the next step was to tell other people. My life changed radically when I did. I wasn't depressed all the time and I didn't have to lie anymore. I could be myself completely. I was no longer afraid that the people I loved "wouldn't like me if they knew who I really was."

By the middle of my senior year, I'd told all my close friends. I also learned how to choose my friends carefully. The crying-myself-to-sleep stopped and my headaches all but vanished. Every time I come out, it gets easier. Much easier. But I still get butterflies in my stomach.

When I came out, I reaffirmed my friendships. True, I lost maybe two friends that way, but most of my friendships got stronger. I proved that it was possible to be out of the closet and still be okay. When I came out, my visibility affected the people around me. The straight people I knew couldn't think about homosexuality in abstract terms anymore. It wasn't about "gays," it was about me, someone they knew. They could deal with me as an individual, and that wasn't so scary.

Step by step I began to love my life. I quit school and came directly to college, where I came out to everyone. Coming out gave me so much self-respect and so much of myself, I barely recognized the introvert I had been when I was in the closet. I even came out to my mother, and she's been incredibly wonderful and supportive.

I won't say that coming out solved all my problems, but it got me out of the personal hell I was living in. And it gave me the strength to deal with everything else. Now I've got an extremely cool life, wonderful friends who love me for who I am and yes!—a kickass boyfriend to share it with.

Yeah, passing for straight is useful when we don't want to deal with discrimination. But every time we hide, we degrade ourselves. If I decide not to hold my boyfriend's hand in public because I don't want to call attention to our gayness, I degrade us both. We deserve to be treated well and to be able to openly express our honest feelings for one another. We should be able to hold hands in public without being ashamed. Being out is something we owe to ourselves, and to others around us. I guess that's propagandistic. But it's honest and that's what matters to me most.

Being gay doesn't define who I am. I am a human being first and foremost. But being gay is an integral and valid part of me—as much as loving writing or music, or liking sci-fi. So I have a boyfriend instead of a girlfriend and I have to worry about discrimination and gay bashing. My life's been a little harder than most. But I've learned more about love and prejudice, and myself than I might have otherwise. All of this is who I am. And I wouldn't have it any other way.

I got way too close to suicide when I was in the closet. I hated my life. I was tired of lying, and of being afraid. I was tired of censoring everything I said, and of the invisible wall between me and the people I loved. One night, I found myself with a knife in my hand, and I thought, "Nothing can hurt more than this." I had to end my pain, either by killing myself or by killing what was hurting me. I realized that I could die anytime, but I could only live once. So I chose to come out. It was difficult, but I did it. And the pain stopped.
It was like breathing for the first time.   — Adam age 19

JOSIE

◑

IT HAS NOW BEEN OVER SIX YEARS THAT I HAVE BEEN OUT TO MYSELF. WHILE I AM ATTEMPT-ING TO SHARE WHAT THIS EXPERIENCE WAS LIKE, PLEASE REALIZE THAT I HAVE A MUCH EAS-IER TIME DESCRIBING FACTS THAN FEELINGS. IN THE BEGINNING OF MY FRESHMAN YEAR IN

high school, I met Gina. To say that we were friends was not enough—it was like a part of me that had been missing had been filled with her in my life. She broke through all of my walls and loved me—baggage and all. Looking back, I was completely in love with her, but I had never made the connection that I could be gay. A few months later, she came out to me. I told her that I didn't care if she was gay and that I was not. I really believed that. I had never been attracted to boys, I just figured that my time had not come. Later on, there was a military ball that the two of us went to with men. Gina's date, a mutual friend of ours, asked her to go out with him and she said yes. My heart broke when she told me later that night. I could not understand why I was so devastated by this news. I wasn't so worried that we would spend less time together. It was something much more powerful.

After a few days I realized I belonged with Gina and not our friend. I had a dream that I kissed her. One night it happened and I knew with the intimacy and intensity of our kiss why I hurt so much at the dance. Then, I freaked out. As much as I was not homophobic about everyone else, I was homophobic about my being gay. I felt that something was really wrong with me. That feeling conflicted greatly with those that I felt for Gina. Why did I care that it was a woman who I was in love with? Why did I know that it would change my life? It was upsetting for me, but I knew that I had to follow my heart. I felt a strange calmness. It was the first time that I had been true to myself in a long time. It is not to say that I did not want to be straight, or that I did not think and talk about it with Gina, but I knew that I was someone who loved other women.

I am proud to say that I love being a woman, that I love being with women, and that I am engaged to a woman. But it would be wonderful not to be known as Josie that lesbian or token dyke. My sexual orientation is a part of me, but it is not all of who I am or what makes me. The rest of my being is not contingent upon whom I fall in love with.

There is a lot of unspoken pressure for people to come out to the world and I think that it is unnecessary. We all have unique situations, and our own way of doing things. I was in the closet for three years and out to only a handful of people. I was not ready to come out any more than that, nor was the situation I was in conducive to doing so. Why bother coming out if you know you might be kicked out of your house, or lose friends? There are a lot of legitimate reasons why we don't come out. On the other hand, there are a lot of gay people and allies who love us for who we are. There is no need to rush coming out to yourself or anyone else. Finding out who you are and being comfortable with yourself is the most important thing. Even if you do not have a group in your area or feel comfortable about going to one, there are free lines that you can call to get information or talk to someone—you don't even have to tell them who you are. You are not alone.

If you are in the closet, know that it will be okay. You are not alone. It took me almost three years of being out to myself before I truly came out to others. That's okay. Don't be harsh on yourself for not being out, or think of yourself as weak or bad. Simply know that your time will come when the door can be opened and you can walk free. Until then, know that you are not alone.

Josie
Age 18

ROB, DON, Q.C., AND CHAYA

◑

WE ARE STUDENTS AT A LARGE UNIVERSITY ON THE EAST COAST AND HAVE ALL DECIDED TO MAKE THE TWO IN TWENTY SPECIAL INTEREST RESIDENTIAL PROGRAM OUR HOME. THIS IS A COLLEGE-SPONSORED ON-CAMPUS LIVING OPTION WHERE GAY,

lesbian, bisexual, transgendered, and heterosexual allies can elect to live on a special floor in a dorm. Its goals include providing a safe and supportive living space for these students and providing an opportunity to work in various ways to promote tolerance on and off campus.

Many people are nervous when they move on the floor because they are unsure what it will be like. Some worry that they will be forced to proclaim their sexual orientation on a high mountain, or take part in political activism. Although some members of the floor have been actively involved in this work or have declared their sexual orientation from a mountaintop (either literally or figuratively), many choose to live more quietly. Each student is given the freedom to be gay, lesbian, bisexual, transgendered, or heterosexual in his or her own way.

Our floor gives students a place to live where they can be open about their sexual orientation without fear of physical or emotional harm. There has been some harassment from people not living on the floor, but the program makes sure that such incidents are not ignored, and overall the number of such harassment has been low.

Here, people can be themselves. We can decorate our rooms as we wish. Some choose to hang a freedom flag or a photo of their partner on the wall. As long as one's roommate does not mind, we are free to create an environment where we feel comfortable and where we do not have to hide who we are. We also get the luxury of being able to talk about things that we might not feel safe or at ease talking about in

another environment. We have countless discussions about coming out to family and friends, gay-related politics, and groaning that if a person has liked the same individual for three months it is perhaps time to actually talk to that person. Many people find that friendships are made quickly and the deep loneliness of life in the closet slowly fades away.

The floor also sponsors social and political activities. We have marched down the street together in gay pride celebrations, spoken out at National Coming Out Day, gone bowling, had some pretty interesting drag balls as well as a variety of other activities. Halloween, for instance, is never boring. Last year a certain history of costume class got quite a surprise when Q. C. showed up in full Victorian elegance.

We have been blessed with a wonderful residents assistant for many semesters. She was forever on call, day or night. She was there when students were disowned because of their sexual orientation. She was there to chat with (provided she was awake). She was there for us every moment of every day. She graduated last semester and as she said good-bye, I marveled at the fact that she was still sane.

Some problems come up on the floor. Residents don't always get along and sometimes roommates have bitter fights. The rooms are small and sometimes people feel cramped for space. Also, Madonna, Melissa Ethridge, and disco can really get on some people's nerves after the ninth run of the same CD. But all in all, most of us find that living on this floor is an incredibly wonderful experience and one that we would not give up for the world.

I'm here, gay, happy, and proud.

Rob
Age: 20

Yo, I'm Don and I'm from Rockland County, N.Y. I'm a gay teenager and I'm butch.

Don
Age: 19

Hey divas of the world. I'm Q.C., that stands for Queeny Chris. Don't let my name fool you... I'm the butch one of the group!!

Chris
Age: 22

This is me and some friends from my floor in my dorm. We are all gay, but boy are we different!

~Chaya "Mge"
age: 19

SHAKA

◗

I WAS BORN IN KINGSTON, JAMAICA, IN THE EARLY SEVENTIES. AS MOST OF THE STEREOTYPES WILL ATTEST, FOR MANY STEREOTYPES DO HAVE A HINT OF TRUTH, JAMAICA IS A HOMOPHO- BIC COUNTRY. GAYS AND LESBIANS ARE NOT LOOKED FAVORABLY UPON ON THAT BEAUTIFUL

Caribbean island. When I was three, my family moved to Liverpool, England, and stayed there for ten years.

When I was nine, I returned to Jamaica for a year. I was already aware that I did not have the same attraction to girls that the other boys did. I had overheard family discussions about the attitude toward homosexuals in Jamaica, and I paid close attention to what was being said, even though none of it was directed toward me. Upon reflection, I realized that even though the attitude in Jamaica was extremely negative, homosexual activity did exist. The actions of gay men and women were frowned upon; effeminate gay men and "manly" women were most scorned.

Back in Liverpool, a small, conservative city north of London, there was no antigay sentiment in the daily interactions between students. This is not to say that homosexuality was freely accepted. Rather, it was not really spoken about, so there was no bad talk or ridiculing of which I was aware.

In 1989 I moved to Boston and I felt restricted. Restricted from being myself. Restricted at home. Restricted at school. Restricted at play. America did not really seem to be the "land of the free" as I had so often heard it called.

My coming out story is one that I am sure many other young kids share. I feel to some extent that I was forced out of the closet.

While in America I would correspond with my exboyfriends in Liverpool and Jamaica (I guess you could say I was an international harlot!) We would fill each other in on our new experiences. Naturally references were made to love and sexual relations. Naturally, too, my stepmother came across this mail. Upon arriving home from school one day, my little sister brutally informed me that I was in trouble. I immediately thought that it had something to do with my sexuality. I ran to my room and, to my horror, discovered that one of my letters was missing. Then I knew for sure. My heart sank to my feet and I was bathed in fear.

I nervously sat on my bed poring over likely responses in my mind to the questions that my parents would ask. "Should I say this, should I say that?" I wondered. They tried to come up with all these cultural reasons for my "state." For example, "Your mother never breast-fed you. Your mother abused you, that's why." They also believed that someone was taking advantage of me and paying me for sex. Not only was I gay now, but a perceived prostitute too. My, my, what a lucky day it was!

My parents questioned my sanity. Then the inevitable statement was uttered: "Well, if you're gay, you can't live in our house."

The next few months were tense. I would stay out later and later, coming home only when I knew my parents were asleep. Eventually I moved out. I never became suicidal or turned to drugs or alcohol, thank God. I tried to network and find other gay kids who were experiencing the same problems. I moved into a group home and from there I built a foundation for my new independence.

Out of the three countries that I lived in, the UK definitely seemed to be the most liberal. However, I was in America and had to adapt to the sentiment here. I observed the different attitudes that each culture had and could see how the population arrived at their bigoted views. Understanding the cultures gave me the strength and security to be myself, rather than being consumed by bigotry.

I'm in the process of molding my personality, seeking out that which is important to me, building a foundation for my new independence. This is an on-going process which gives me the strength and security to persevere and build both myself and my community.

xx Shubu oo   Age 22
☺ ☺

MOLLIE

◐

MANY ESSENTIAL COMPONENTS MAKE UP MY PERSONALITY AND SOUL. I HAVE BEEN AN AVID FLUTIST FOR OVER TEN YEARS, PARTICIPATING IN A VARIETY OF MUSICAL GROUPS, AND THROUGH ONE OF THEM I WAS ABLE TO TRAVEL TO JAPAN. I STAYED IN the homes of three different Japanese families and got a wonderful taste of Japanese life, a culture extremely different from my own.

Traveling is a very solid part of my existence. Having been on several trips to the Caribbean, Central America, Canada, and Europe, I have gained a deeper cultural understanding of the world around me. I believe I have a greater acceptance for people who are different from me, and those differences help me understand more about myself.

Although I am a lesbian and I often take an active role in helping to make my community safer for my gay peers, it is a small but significant part of who I am. For me, being a lesbian is like being a woman: I was born a woman, and I am proud of who I am.

Many people have asked me what it is like to grow up as a lesbian. Well what is it like growing up het-erosexual or Asian or Native American or Swedish or Mormon? Just because I happen to be part of a minority does not mean that I feel any different from anyone else.

Although I am not affected in a significant way because of my homosexuality, there are still small sit-uations that should not exist. For example, when I came out three years ago, I received a phone call from an individual who said, "You are a f——ing dyke! Get out of our high school!" I am sure a heterosexual person at my school has never encountered this type of situation. If people are against homosexuality, that is fine. I cannot judge them on the basis of their beliefs. But when a person takes action, either physi-cally or verbally, that's crossing the line. It would be best if all people could understand and learn from those who are different.

I came out to my parents and brother when I was fifteen and in the ninth grade. The first thing my dad said was, "So what's the problem?" I didn't think he would be against it, but his comment made me feel even better about myself. My mom had a similar reaction, but she also spoke of the worry she had for me. She wanted me to be safe. My brother was also very supportive and understanding. I am very grateful to all of them.

Mollie, 17

MICHAEL

◑

Twenty-two years ago my family emigrated to the United States from the impoverished Azores islands in search of a better way of life. My dad got a job at one of the textile factories in our town and my mom stayed home and took care of us kids. I attended a Portuguese parochial school for nine years. I was well liked by my teachers, always did my work, and never got into trouble—the "perfect student." My peers respected my work and I had friends. Looking back on those early years I often feel sorry for myself. Yeah, my teachers liked me and I had friends, but I wasn't happy. Something was not quite right.

When I was about eight years old, I started becoming aware of the things going on around me. For the first time I sensed that there was something different about me. To complicate things even more, my father was an alcoholic. He was verbally and physically abusive. When I was nine years old, my father called me a faggot for the first time. Those words crushed me forever. I ran to my bedroom and cried myself to sleep. I vowed never to forgive him for that.

As I entered adolescence I started to notice the other boys in my class. In history I would find myself fantasizing about the boy sitting in front of me. During the whole week of sex education when we learned about the male anatomy, I was barely able to control my excitement. By now I felt sure that I was attracted to boys and not girls.

In college I had my first sexual experience—it was with a woman. That experience changed my life. I reasoned that I should have enjoyed my experience with her but I didn't. Maybe I was G-A-Y.

In the summer of that same year, I had my first gay sexual experience . . . It was with my cousin. He was married at the time but not very happily. I had suspicions that he might be gay. So one hot August night when I was staying at his house I snuck over to where he was sleeping. I can remember the adrenaline rushing through my veins as I tiptoed to his bedside. He awoke astonished to the touch of my chilled hands across his stomach. Ashamed I quickly snuck out and went back to bed.

Over the course of the next year we met several times. By then he'd left his wife and had come out. Nothing ever came of our relationship because I was too busy feeling guilty about what I was doing. I know now that deep inside what I really wanted was someone to talk to. He proved true to the task. We became very close. I practically lived at his house. By the end of the year he helped me come out. I owe a great debt to him and I love him very much.

Coming out was difficult. My biggest obstacle was overcoming guilt. I couldn't help feeling ashamed. I kept having this image of my mother looking down at me in disapproval and disgust. She had never accepted anything I did, at least she never told me so.

I'd never really known what it was like to love or be loved. My parents weren't very expressive. My mom and dad never told me they loved me. They assumed that I knew it. They never expressed their love for one another either. Therefore, I felt unequipped with the skills needed to love and be loved. When someone came along who actually loved me, it seemed alien.

I'm in a long-term relationship now. My boyfriend and I have been together for two years. As much as I fight to deny it, I love him. We've gone through a lot together and have shared many wonderful and some not so wonderful times. We've learned a lot from each other. He's taught me to like and to believe in myself. He's helped me to express my feelings. And most important, he taught me how to love.

Unfortunately my parents have not yet come to terms with my sexual orientation. Therefore when I am at home, I feel the need to hide the fact that I'm gay. This makes going home then not so welcoming. I feel jealous that I can't openly talk about my relationship with my boyfriend to my parents, in the same way my sister can. It hurts me that my dad and I can't have a relationship aside from talking about cars. I often find myself thinking about the times when dad and I would work side by side every night in the garden. What saddens and scares me most of all is the thought of dying and never having been able to share such a large part of my life with my parents.

— Michael, 22

CRAIG

❶

EVER SINCE I CAME OUT OF THE CLOSET ALMOST THREE YEARS AGO, AT THE AGE OF FIF-
TEEN, I HAVE NEVER BEEN ASHAMED OF MY SEXUALITY. I GREW UP KNOWING I WAS HOMO-
SEXUAL AND I GREW UP STRONG, INSIDE. I KNEW I WASN'T GOING TO KEEP SUCH A BIG
part of who I am a secret forever.

Since kindergarten I have had crushes on guys. In fourth grade I secretly fell in love with my best friend. My love lasted eight years. He and I never actually had a relationship but our friendship was more than anybody could ever fathom. Imagine loving somebody so close to you, so much, and you could never touch that person, kiss him, or hold him with the intimacy you need when you're in love. Imagine never being able to say I love you.

I think nothing of the fact that I came out at fif-teen. I just wanted to be free. Coming out of the closet is like a butterfly hatching from its cocoon. As a caterpillar it is young and primarily defenseless. As it matures it is preparing to show the world its true colors. It forms a cocoon and for a time it remains there, awaiting the day when it can come out. The cocoon finally hatches and a new creature comes forth. A little shaky at first, the butterfly spreads its marvelous wings and takes off into flight. No longer burdened by the hardships of gravity, it sets out upon a new life and it is free.

I am a human being. I have thoughts and feelings, skin and bone. I also have talents, just like everybody. My sexuality is not me but it's a big part of me. We're all capable of falling in love and nobody has the right or power to say I can't fall in love with a man. It shouldn't matter who I choose to love. I have a mind of my own and now it's stronger than ever. I'm here, I'm queer, and it's my life!

Craig -16-

THORA

◐

I WAS FOURTEEN WHEN I REALIZED THAT MY STRONG FEELINGS TOWARD MY OWN SEX WERE PROBABLY NOT JUST ONES OF "REALLY LIKING WOMEN." I ACTUALLY FELL IN LOVE WITH THEM AND WANTED MORE FROM FEMALES THAN THE USUAL BUSINESS OF TALKING, HUGGING, OR

going to the movies together. I felt more alone than words can describe, sort of like I was living all by myself on an isolated piece of rock in the ocean with no sign of land or another living being around. I frequently cried myself to sleep, whispering, "I'm a lesbian." I tried repeatedly to convince myself that I was heterosexual by focusing my attention on guys I thought were at least good-looking and fun to be with. I prayed that my feelings would change. During long nights of insomnia and anxiety, I wondered "Maybe it's just that I haven't met Mr. Right yet, maybe my taste is really different from what most women prefer." At the same time, I couldn't help fantasizing about being close to the woman I was in love with.

In my everyday life I tried to partake in my girlfriends' discussions about boys and I even put some posters of famous men on my wall. But still, I felt very different and didn't dare tell anyone why. I hated myself and thought I looked as bad as I felt, which was pretty ugly and depressed. A few months before I turned sixteen, I got hold of a magazine featuring interviews with several lesbians talking openly about their lives and love for women. A totally new dimension opened up to me. I read it through several times with my hands shaking and my heart beating at least two hundred times a minute. My perception of things changed dramatically. Shortly after that I told my sister and my best friend I was a lesbian. I don't think I'll ever forget the intense feelings of paranoia and fear of rejection. But I actually survived the whole thing.

I joined a gay and lesbian organization and in a few months everyone who was a part of my private life knew about me. I vividly remember going to my first ladies' night at the local lesbian and gay community center. It was a very strange experience indeed. Even though I knew I wanted to be with a woman myself, it still felt awkward to see them kiss one another and dance intimately as if it were the most natural thing in the world. I soon got over that stage and spent the next three years "on the gay scene," socializing a lot at the bar, dancing, and exploring contact with different kinds of women. It was great to finally feel like I belonged somewhere. I could be myself, and without a doubt going to the center was a very important step for me in connecting with my sexuality, learning to understand it, and loving myself as a lesbian. Eventually I got tired of that scene and I decided to move on. I had lost contact with some of my old friends and I was missing a clear sense of my needs and wants in life, regardless of my sexual orientation. So, instead of being "busy being a lesbian," I switched over to being "busy being a person."

I discovered that I don't need to hang around in specific places, drink lots of alcohol, or sleep with somebody I don't love or who doesn't love me in order to meet a partner. I can meet wonderful gay, lesbian, and bisexual people wherever I go because there are plenty of us around!

My sexuality is a part of my identity today but not the thing that runs my life, and that feels appropriate for me. I believe that the need to love and to be loved is what connects us all at the very core, and I imagine there being as many different ways of expressing that reality as there are people in the world.

I believe that my soul speaks to me through the voice of my heart and that by following it I will stay happy. I'm certainly not going to put up any walls around my identity that would limit my self-expression by clinging to roles or ideas. So far I've experienced myself as a lesbian — isn't that great!

♡ Thora, age 22

ERIC

❂

I USED TO CORRESPOND WITH TONS OF PEOPLE THROUGH PRODIGY AND AMERICA ONLINE. THE COMPUTER ALLOWS YOU TO MEET PEOPLE IN A SAFE ENVIRONMENT. I MET MY FIRST BOYFRIEND WHEN I WAS FIFTEEN THROUGH THE COMPUTER. WE TALKED ON THE PHONE A LOT and eventually met. To make a long story short, we fell in love.

My parents started to ask a lot of questions. They wanted to know why I was hanging out so much with this guy. Eventually the questions got on my nerves and I decided to tell them. Right off the bat they told me that they would do whatever it took to support me. Fortunately they have had gay friends. The only major problem was that I started to feel uncomfortable around my dad because I knew it made him somewhat uncomfortable. Over time, things with him have gotten much better.

Although I was a junior in high school, I attended GLB meetings at the local college and was soon asked to speak to an adolescent psychology class and I continued to do so for the next two years. Through the college group, I went to the March on Washington where I was interviewed by FOX TV for a new show, *Front Page*. They were airing a segment on gay and lesbian youth and if I agreed to be interviewed, it would mean coming out to everyone. At the time it seemed like the biggest decision I would ever make. No one had ever come out in my school, much less gone on national television. But I figured, it was my last year, and the people I cared about the most were already standing behind me. So I did it. And one Saturday night in early October, almost every kid in my high school was watching *Front Page* to see why Eric was on TV.

I definitely made the right decision. I didn't experience any hassles, threats, or violence. In fact, I made new friends and received recognition and admiration. I am proud of who I am and it doesn't matter anymore what other people think. I'll come out to anyone. I've got a loving family, and terrific friends, and it's their opinion and acceptance that matters, nothing else.

Coming out of the closet doesn't just happen overnight, it's a process that you will be dealing with for the rest of your life. With every person you meet, you will have to make the decision whether to come out to them. It's up to you to decide if you feel safe coming out and if it's appropriate, or even necessary. It's important to realize that your family and friends will also go through an understanding process. You have to be patient and willing to offer them as much information as you can. Remember that the older generation wasn't exposed to homosexuality or even informed about it as much as we are today. So they too, need time to learn and accept it.

I had to develop courage and strength to come out and a lot of it came from my parents. They are strong and intelligent individuals, and raised me to believe in myself and what I stand for. They always taught me to do what's right for me. So when I felt ready to come out, I did it for myself and not for anyone else. My parents' acceptance was the most important thing to me, and receiving it really made me strong.

Growing up gay is an extraordinary experience that many teenagers have to face. It can be a heavy burden, but still it's possible to overcome and live a happy and productive life. For me, it's been both positive and negative. At first I had a loss of confidence in myself and felt hopeless in many instances. I thought that gay people couldn't grow up and enjoy full lives.

Being gay has taught me a lot too. It has given me a chance to grow in ways I don't think other teenagers can. It has given me strength and determination to overcome anything and has made me a stronger individual. I've found I'm less dependent on other people and more on myself. Being gay has opened my eyes to the world so now I can really appreciate people's uniqueness and diversity. This means I can love people no matter what label they have been given.

Eric age 17

JENNIFER

◐

GROWING UP, I COULD SENSE THAT I WAS NOT QUITE WHAT I WAS EXPECTED TO BE, BUT I DIDN'T UNDERSTAND WHY. FOR INSTANCE, UNTIL I WAS FIVE AND A HALF, I HAD LONG HAIR. I DIDN'T LIKE BRUSHING IT. FINALLY, MY MOM THREATENED TO CUT IT ALL OFF. I

took her up on the offer, refusing to brush my hair at all. Eventually she took the scissors out.

I remember going to my grandparents' house for a family picnic a few weeks later. My uncle asked my mother where she'd gotten that little boy, referring to me. I didn't know how to react. This situation has repeated itself throughout my life. "This is the ladies' room. Shouldn't you be in the other bathroom?"

I didn't like to wear dresses. I liked to play sports. At recess I played football with the boys. However, I didn't exactly fit in with the boys either. Sometimes I would go over my best friend's house and play nerf football and hang out. I liked spending time with him. Then he asked me to "Go Out" with him. I said no. The whole thing scared the hell out of me. After that he stopped hanging out with me.

The girls didn't like me because I didn't do girl things. The boys didn't like me because I didn't want to hold their hands or kiss them. I didn't feel close to anyone. I didn't know why it was that I felt so alone.

I had only heard of lesbians in bad jokes. The older I got the more uncomfortable I became when the word was mentioned, not knowing it would eventually refer to me.

Once, representatives from my high school were sent to a workshop on diversity. An acquaintance of mine had been one of the students to participate. My math teacher asked her about the experience in class one day. I remember that she mentioned homosexuality. She didn't really have anything to say about it because there were possibly one or two guys who *maybe were* gay in our high school and, she said, "There are certainly no dykes." I had never heard the word "dyke" before. Dyke Dyke Dyke. I wasn't quite sure what it meant, but I felt myself look down, avoiding all eyes, feeling like they were all directed at me. Dyke.

I was the dyke and hadn't known it. Around this time I finally made a good friend. I liked when her hand would brush against mine, when she would sit close to me and speak softly, allowing me to trust her. I didn't think of kissing her. I'd never seen two women kiss. I'd rarely seen women hold hands. However, had she brought it up, I would have kissed her in a moment.

It didn't happen, though. She got a boyfriend and stopped spending time with me. I was insanely jealous of him. It wasn't until college that I realized I had been in love with her. The pieces finally started coming together then. I met women who weren't afraid to love women. Homosexuality was something beautiful, not something to hide. When I realized I was queer, it made sense to me. The past made sense too.

I am out to all my friends, but I am not directly out to my family. They seem to know that I am a lesbian, but the words have not been said. We've never been communicative. I don't feel at home with them.

At a family gathering a few years ago, my grandmother said with obvious distaste that women who shave their heads are dykes. I was very surprised to hear the word "dyke" come out of her mouth. Last spring I shaved my head, coincidentally before another family gathering. That time nobody mentioned dykes or women with shaved heads, although my grandmother did indicate later that I shouldn't worry about not having a boyfriend yet—I still had time. I have wondered what their thoughts were about me, but in my family's home such things are not spoken about. Their home is not mine. I am not what they expected, not what they wanted. So now, I surround myself with friends, seeking to live in a supportive atmosphere and hoping that as time passes, my sense of home will strengthen.

I make large puppets and masks. I am attempting to create a giant paper-mache circus. Giant purple and green gender-ambiguous giraffes tango to cello accompaniment, creating a world clearly outside of our everyday grasp. I hope to challenge people's established sense of reality with this beautiful, wondrous world and help them to see that everyone doesn't fit into the norm. It's important that the difference of each individual be embraced without being perceived as unnatural or dangerous. Difference can open our eyes to beauty.

— Jen (age 20)

MYCROFT

❶

I FEEL A PERSONAL AND A PROFESSIONAL DUTY TO SPEAK DIRECTLY TO TRANSGENDERED AND QUESTIONING YOUTH, BEING A TRANSGENDERED PERSON AND AN EDUCATOR ON THE SUBJECT. TO THEM I SAY THIS: IT'S BEST TO BE YOURSELF, PEOPLE WILL LIKE YOU FOR WHO YOU ARE,

and those who don't have a problem. Everyone is special and different. It is good to be transgendered—the fact that some people think it's bad or wrong doesn't make it so; a lot of people, transgendered and not, are our allies, and their number is growing every day. You can be transgendered *and* have a happy life—do what you want, be out, have a relationship, have a family. If you're male, you can dress like a woman and/or be one; if you're a female, you can dress like a man and/or be one. I believed all this was true before I came out, and now I *know* it's true because I've seen it and lived it.

By sixth grade I was a female who identified as a man, and that was pretty much okay with my friends, but other kids thought I was "weird," even though it was okay to be unique. Junior high was very different. There was a lot of pressure to be straight and "normal"—to dress right, date, and gossip. My school friends were into that and tried to help me get with it. At school I tried to be a feminine straight girl; my friends knew I disliked being that way and most of the guys harassed me. Outside of school I was a straight boy; I had different friends who pretty much accepted me.

I knew that outside of school I was the real me, the person I wanted to be as an adult. In each life I didn't want to think about the other one; I couldn't really deal with my double life or what it might mean. I didn't know of any support for GLBT youth at that time. I just had a few friends and teachers who accepted me but didn't know how to talk about it.

I came out in high school, first as a lesbian, then as transgendered: a straight female-to-male transsexual. I came out because I needed to be honest—with myself and the people I knew. I also came out to help other GLBT youth—especially those who are transgendered.

I love being transgendered and am proud of it, and I wouldn't wish to be any other way. I am happy and successful in many things. I have been able to do something positive for GLBT youth including being part of this photo project. My portrait and words travel the country in an exhibit and now in this book.

If I can do it, so can you. And you can do it with pride, and you can do it differently and better. You have no one to prove yourself to except you.

I believe that it is my right, & everyone's right to express themselves fully & freely, as long as they're happy & not hurting anyone. As a transgendered man (a straight female-to-male transsexual), I have the right to express my identity & my pride like anyone else, especially along with my gay, lesbian & bisexual family.

For as long as I can remember, my primary role model has been Sherlock Holmes (et al.), so if I want to be or look like a really old-fashioned man, that should be cool; because I love it & I'm not doing anything wrong. Anyone should be able to talk about their experience & be listened to, believed, & learned from. Each person's experience is valid & real for them, & adds to the total of human knowledge & diversity.

Mycroft Age 20

RACHEL

◗

FOURTEEN YEARS OLD, I AM SITTING ON A PARK BENCH IN LOS ANGELES. MY BEST FRIEND IS SITTING ON THE GROUND, AND HER HAIR IS DRAPED AROUND MY THIGHS AND CATCHES THE CALIFORNIA SUN AS SHE FIDGETS. SOMEONE IS TELLING HER AN OUTRAGEOUS STORY.

She laughs when she finishes and looks up at me. Her eyes are round, her mouth a wet garnet red, its natural color; and I am intensely aware of her shoulders, strong from swimming, against my legs. I catch her cheeks in my hands, hold her face in my gaze for some time. I want to kiss her, but instead I smile and release her.

Later the man who is with us in the park asks if I have any inclinations toward women. I explain that I have never really thought about it, and remind him of the boy I am seeing at home. He looks at me for a minute, and I admit that I am very attracted to my friend on the bench. When I return home in a week, I stop seeing my boyfriend. It just doesn't seem right.

My attraction for my friend grows, becomes almost a plague—though a rather pleasant one. That is my last year in high school, and I lose my virginity to a male friend I'm not dating. It is something I want to do before going to college, but I don't want a relationship with him, not while I am still in love with my friend.

In March I am reading the paper at her kitchen table, and she tells me about a writing assignment in which she is to come up with ten things she would do if she found out she only had a short time to live. She tells me she would make love to her best friend (a man). I can't face her. I read the paper more intently and say, "So would I." She changes the subject.

At college I am involved with several women, and one man. The women are fleeting (even though I will always be more attracted to women) but the man is constant. He especially understands that I couldn't pass up the chance to be with my best friend. Sometimes people won't take my orientation seriously because of him.

I am not unique in my bisexuality, but I don't announce it to the world either. In my freshman composition class I write an essay reflecting on a past experience to examine why I am how I am today. I write about my father, and why I haven't come out to him yet. The next day, my professor, a very nice man with three kids, crinkled eyes, and a beard, asks if I would mind if he reads my draft to the class. I look around the room at fourteen people with whom I have yet to have any serious conversations, wipe my rapidly perspiring palms on my jeans, and say, "Uhf, sure, go ahead." I swallow hard. I try to smile, but I think I fail. My professor reads my piece slowly and very richly. It is lovely. The class critiques my writing, asks a few questions about my father, suggests I continue with the piece and "explore further" my feelings of ambivalence about coming out.

And I do. The next semester I write and produce a play in part about bisexuality. Through working on that, I end up announcing my orientation to the student body and the faculty. But I still can't get myself to come out to my parents. It just seems too awkward. When I return to school at the beginning of my sophomore year, I print out a copy of my play and leave it in a prominent place in my parents' house. I assume that they'll read it, but they never say anything about it to me. A few months later, I need their permission to do this project. I explain that it is a project focusing on positive images of "gay youths," as I term myself to my father. He asks if it will say that I am a "gay youth." I start to explain, but my mother, on the other extension, remembers the boyfriend I have been talking about recently and beats me to what I am about to say: "Bisexual, dear." I am dumbfounded. My mother has the nerve to say the word I am too scared to say to her.

I want to see teachers acknowledge that non-heterosexual orientations are significant and relevant. These issues belong in course materials for literature, art, psychology, history (everything except perhaps math). It is extremely important to recognize that queer issues are a part of everyday life for a large number of people. For us, this not only validates our experience, but also reflects the world more accurately. For myself, I want people to know that I am who I am (not _what_ I am). This means not only that I _am_ a bisexual woman, but that I _am_ a lot of other things as well, all important to me, but none definitive. No one should forget my intelligence, talents, or interests because of the company I keep.

Rachel, 17

NATHAN

◐

IN THE BOTTOM OF A BUNK BED, WITH MY BROTHER ABOVE ME ASLEEP, I LAY THINKING ABOUT WHY I WAS DIFFERENT. ALL THE OTHER BOYS HAD CRUSHES ON MEGAN AND KELLY. WHY DID I HAVE A CRUSH ON MICHAEL? I HAD NO NAME FOR MY FEELINGS AND I FELT ALONE. IT WASN'T until seventh grade that I found out I wasn't alone, and I realized that I would be fine. Still, as much as I wasn't alone in the world, I was alone in myself. After all, I was still in the closet.

I really began to feel the need to come out in the next few years. The longer I waited, the more angry, agitated, nervous, and edgy I became. I was so miserable that neither my family nor my friends wanted to be around me. There was so much good inside that just needed to come out but it was all trapped behind that closet door.

In September of my sophomore year in high school, I came out to my family. That was the first and hardest step. Of course I expected it to be all peaches and cream, but let's face it, it took me sixteen years to come to terms with my sexual orientation, I couldn't demand that they do it overnight.

Throughout my childhood, my parents raised me to understand my own worth and value. With their help I have grown enough to know how to express everything about myself—whether it be my sexual orientation, my opinion on gay rights, or anything else. If my parents had not taught me to speak up for myself and my rights I am certain my life would not be half as easy as it is today. Everyone needs to find the freedom and joy that comes with self-expression. When I opened the door to the person who was trapped, repressed inside of me, I found my true self. As scary as it may seem, coming out of the closet is probably one of the greatest experiences in a gay, lesbian, or bisexual person's life. All my misery, pain, and confusion came to an end. Coming out made all my relationships stronger and freed my spirit. It was the first step in my acceptance of myself. My life was no longer ruled by a lie.

I have always felt a beautiful safety in being myself. There was once a time that I, like so many others, wore a mask to create a me that I thought would be perfect for society. When I finally came out, I was able to shed that mask and reflect on what I had created. Not only was my shedded creation a carbon copy of everyone I knew, it was also a hideous portrait of all that I never wanted to be. Once I saw the strength and beauty of the real me, I felt safer than I ever had before. When I found truth in myself, I found safety in my world.

My parents' underlying love for each other and their children is the standard I have set for my own life. Everything they do is filled with love, their marriage, their children, their lives. They are a true example of a union of souls. My husband's and my love for each other and our marriage will be like theirs. How, having seen it work, could I settle for anything else?

What inspires me most about my parents and our family is that our happiness did not come easily. We had to actively fight to be as happy as we are today. I think that gives me a better appreciation for all that we have. My parents are both my inspiration and my role models because they continue to love no matter what life brings them. I thank my dad and mom everyday of my life for showing me what real love and a real family are. My vision is to have a secure life with a home, a husband, children, and a family of my own to create memories with.
I am no different than you.

Nathan
age 20

JAYSON

◐

IGREW UP IN A RURAL TOWN IN VERMONT LIVING ON ASSISTANCE FROM THE GOVERNMENT FOR TWELVE YEARS. MY PARENTS WERE DIVORCED WHEN I WAS SIX MONTHS OLD, AND THREE YEARS LATER MY MOTHER REMARRIED. SHE DID THE BEST THAT SHE COULD TO RAISE HER three children.

My mother is the biggest inspiration in my life. I hope to have the dedication and courage for life that she does. She has taught me to stand up for all I believe in and never to let anyone walk on me. She believes in me, and even though she is having difficulty understanding that I am gay, I know that one day she will be able to accept me for who I am. Since I was photographed for this project, she has made small steps toward accepting me in my entirety. She has recently confirmed that she will stand by me no matter what.

I now understand why my mother's initial reaction to my gayness was so harsh. Throughout her life she was inundated with negative stereotypes about gay men and she didn't want me to struggle. She wanted me to have a white picket fence around my house on a hill, and all of the other things she did not have in her life. When I came out to her, her vision of what my life would be was shattered. It became my job to pick up the pieces and to rebuild that picture. I am and I will be successful. At school I have already assumed many leadership positions. I have kept my grades high, worked hard, and proven to her that I am still the same boy she cradled in her arms. Most of all I have proven to myself that I can do it. I can do anything.

I was fortunate to be elected junior and senior class president at my high school as an openly gay-bisexual male. In order to achieve this, I worked hard to show people the positive aspects of my personality. I demonstrated my enthusiasm, dedication and responsibility to the highest degree. This showed ~~my~~ my classmates that I was multifaceted and that being gay was just one of my positive qualities.

Most of my friends have a positive attitude about my sexuality and were not surprised when I confirmed their suspicions. My parents on the other hand, have rejected the possibility that I might be gay. They suggest that I am confused or "going through a phase." They have warned that if I confirm my sexuality as anything other than heterosexual, I will be disowned.

Jayson, age 18

LEAH

◐

MY FAMILY'S DINNER TOPICS REVOLVED AROUND POLITICS EVER SINCE I WAS EXTREMEMLY YOUNG. WHO WAS RUNNING AGAINST WHOM, WHAT ACT JUST GOT VOTED ON AND THE ABILITIES OF SENATOR SO AND SO. AFTER A CONGRESSIONAL INTERNSHIP

in Washington, D.C., when I was sixteen, I decided that I could do a better job and I set my sights on being a U.S. senator. But I had this notion in my thick head that being gay meant having to slip off to the sides of society. I would never be able to venture into politics as I wanted. Who would vote for a Korean-American lesbian woman? Coming out would alter all my life plans. I was not only afraid of lack of acceptance in future voting booths, but also with present friends at college.

A couple of my closest friends are Asian American and straight. I have known them since our first years at college. We griped about men and reluctantly I went with them to frat parties. I was extremely concerned about what would happen after I came out. Would they feel betrayed by my being gay? Would I feel betrayed by them if they didn't accept me for being queer? For a while, I thought I couldn't be gay because I didn't know of any gay Asians. I also assumed that to be a lesbian, one had to dress and act a certain way: short hair, motorcycle jacket and no up-front sense of humor. All of these factors made it hard for me to take the step.

It felt as though coming out would be the most traumatic event of my life. I came out to friends, by announcing it and then taking it back the next day. I am not quite sure what I was afraid of; I always believed that I was a straight ally who had many gay friends. I guess that even though I had been around queer people for a while, I was a closet homophobic.

Coming out has made me a whole person. I am more confident than when I was deliberately hiding my sexual orientation. I wasted so much energy denying my feelings and avoiding thinking about women sexually. I have kept straight Asian friends, but I have also lost some other friends, not because I changed but because they did.

The most important step in coming out was realizing that although I am gay, that didn't mean I had to change. I am aware that there are other Asian lesbians and that we are gaining a strong voice. I am also aware that I can be involved in politics and that if I want to, hell, I *can* be a U.S. senator.

I am not going to change or apologize for who I am. It's the society that needs to change. American society is trying so hard to shame me for how I feel towards another human being. I will not be shamed!

Leah 21

CHRIS

◐

I WAS THE YOUNGEST OF FIVE CHILDREN BORN TO IRISH IMMIGRANTS. MY PARENTS' VALUE SYSTEM WAS BASED IN THE CATHOLIC CHURCH. MY FATHER, AT TIMES, WAS VERY ABUSIVE TO MY MOTHER AND SIBLINGS, AND DURING HIS TIRADES HE WOULD OFTEN SCREAM ABOUT KILLING

faggots. I was barely six when this was happening and my mother would try as best she could to shield me—she became my sole support at an early age.

It was around this time that my feelings of difference began to surface. I had some sense of what being gay meant and I was beginning to get crushes on some of my male friends. This caused a lot of pain and confusion. I already had an idea that I would be punished if I let anyone know about these feelings. My father's homophobia became very blatant when two of my siblings came out within a few months of each other. My parents disowned them both and my father began to refer to them as "the faggots." My mother's heartache and grief became apparent and I quickly tried to suppress my feelings toward boys.

As if the home problems weren't bad enough, my parents enrolled me in Catholic school. I spent years feeling isolated and was repeatedly taught that I was different and unworthy of acceptance. During childhood I tried to change so that I could belong. Incidents of cruelty, homophobia, and violence were constant. By junior high I had suffered through several breakdowns alone and had begun to pray for death.

The beginning of my high school experience was worse. I attended an all-boys Catholic high school. Unbearable homophobia began again on both a personal and systematic level, even though I was still denying my sexual orientation. I was beginning to numb and feel indifferent to the prejudice surrounding me. The more I drew into myself, the more I liked the person I was on the inside. The more comfortable I became with myself the more my peers tried to break my spirit. They attempted this with both physical violence and death threats at school and at home.

It was because of these threats that I was outed to my mother. She took me aside one night and asked me if I was gay and although it took some time, she accepted me. This was the most awakening and free-

ing experience and it showed me I wasn't a bad person. With this new freedom I sought help from the administration at my school. They were unresponsive and blatantly homophobic and suggested that I act a little less gay and try sports. Ultimately they suggested that I look for another school since they were neither prepared or willing to deal with my "problem." I walked out and never went back.

I began to seek out other youths in my position in order to cope. I found them at a group called BAGLY (The Boston Alliance of Gay and Lesbian Youth). This group changed my life. I learned to accept myself and to have pride in the gay community and its history. For once I was able to discover who I was without the pressures or prejudices of others.

I was asked to speak on behalf of the gay and lesbian students' rights bill and suddenly I was an activist. I was speaking at rallies, schools, and the state house. I began to see how the complex issues of sexism, classism, and racism affected both my life and society. I appeared in several books, magazines, and papers and made television appearances locally and nationally. I was drunk with the attention but in the process lost my true purpose. Eventually I couldn't handle politics anymore and dropped it all and tried to be a normal teen.

Being open about my sexual orientation has tried my inner strength and my ability to face prejudice. Coming out also gave me the opportunity to educate and support a range of people, often without trying. Support is crucial. A friend, priest, or maybe even a member of your family can help you feel safe being who you are so you can solve some of your own problems. Then you can become a support to someone else.

Being comfortable with myself allows people to see that being gay isn't a bad thing and that gay kids are no different from other kids. I have the usual worries of someone my age: making time for my boyfriend, getting money for school, and finding a place to fit in.

As much as it hurts and feels unfair, it is often times necessary for me to hide who I am. It is not easy to be gay and grow up in a primarily Catholic working class neighborhood. Even a simple trip to the store can become dangerous when people believe you are gay. You have to develop a straight act just to survive. Being an activist didn't make my situation any easier. People didn't just think I was gay, they knew it and worse yet, I was an uppity fag. While this made the retribution worse, it provided me with an outlet to combat homophobia. It allowed me to face the taunts with my head held high and hold the knowledge that I was doing something to make it easier for future generations of queer youth.

Chris, 19

DOMINIQUE

◐

I DON'T WANT SPECIAL RIGHTS FOR WHO I AM. I JUST WANT THE RIGHTS I DO HAVE TO BE ENFORCED. I DO NOT WANT TO BE DISCRIMINATED AGAINST.

BY BEING OUT I'M ALLOWING PEOPLE TO KNOW I EXIST. I AM EDUCATING THEM ABOUT BEING diverse in my choice of lifestyle. I am informing them that their ignorance toward me and others needs to stop! What was it like before I came out? I felt like a part of myself was hidden from the ones I loved. I was trapped, confused, and stressed out. I didn't have the strength to tell my friends, family, or myself I was a lesbian.

My message to everyone is: Know people for their names and what is in their hearts, not their sexual preference, race, religion, or even by a disease they might have, that's what the world needs.

My mother would deny me by not speaking to me for three months at a time, which made me want to give living. I tried to commit suicide to end the pain. After, I got out of the hospital, I came to Massachusetts to live with my father. He claimed to understand the issues in my life. Five months later, however, I found myself in foster care, because instead of understanding he tried to beat the homosexuality out of me.

Somehow I remained strong and was blessed with a pretty good foster mother, but I was harassed at my high school and almost got jumped for being a lesbian. I was moved again to a new foster home. Now I have two lesbian mothers and a family who accepts me for me. I feel safe with my family but still open to society's abuse.

—Dominique, 17

EDUAL

◐

I WISH I COULD SAY I CAME OUT BECAUSE I FELT EMPOWERED, BUT THAT WOULDN'T BE TELLING THE TRUTH. I CAME OUT BECAUSE I WAS CONFRONTED BY MY MOM. I HAD COME OUT TO MY SISTER, EMELIN, A YEAR EARLIER. MONTHS LATER, MY SISTER

trusted her friend, Renee, with our secret. But eventually, Emelin and I were both betrayed under the pretense of moral obligation. Renee, now the ex-best friend, made sure her mom got wind of this juicy little tidbit too.

Renee's mom felt the moral obligation to inform my mom as well as several other good friends.

We knew none of this until one day, while sitting in our white station wagon, waiting for the traffic light to turn green, my mom blurted out, "Your sister's best friend's mother tells me that you're a homosexual. (Trust me, it rolls much better in Spanish.) Is that true?"

My reality came to a complete standstill at that moment. I mean *everything* froze, including my heart. I was speechless. As I debated what course of action to take, I looked in the back seat of our station wagon. My sister sat there looking out the window, crying silently.

"Is that true?" my mom repeated, snapping me out of my daze. And in a shaky voice I responded, "Yes, it's true. I'm gay." I wished all hell had broken loose. Instead, my mom just stared at me. She muttered one or two things to herself and then began to drive. My mom is a Jehovah's Witness. Their belief is that homosexuals will be condemned during Armageddon, and may never be granted eternal life in paradise. Because of these convictions, my mom,

no matter how much she loved me, would later turn her back on me. The silence she maintained as she drove screamed at me of my loss. I've lost her forever. My life as I knew it ended in that white station wagon, on that sunny day in Paterson, New Jersey, I thought so anyway. My life really ended when we got home.

My dad was already home when we got there. My mom made me sit down in the living room, where my dad was watching some Spanish television program. She turned to my dad and said, "Dear husband, did you know that your son is a homosexual?" My dad was in complete shock. After what seemed hours, he got up and walked out of the living room. My mom went after him. They came back. My dad asked how could his only son be gay.

Either see a therapist, or leave home. Those were the two choices I was given. I opted for leaving home. So the summer before my eighteenth birthday I left.

It has taken several years to find my niche in society. In those years I learned what the consequences of leaving home really meant. I am happy with the decision that I made but only because I was willing and able to deal with the consequences.

I recommend that anyone thinking of coming out carefully consider what are the best and worst possible outcomes and ask yourself if you are ready to deal with either one.

I wish I grew up eating ham & cheese sandwiches, but I didn't. I ate rice & beans, mole con tortillas, sweet plantains, and huevos rancheros. I used to pretend I was an American who only spoke, but I wasn't. I'm a bilingual, tricultural Mexican-Puerto Rican-American. So trying to figure out what I stand for, and what I believe in has been confusing. I've had to struggle with my whole identity, not just being gay, and it's that process of struggling that makes me feel proud to be out and open. As Sandra Cisneros says, "I've put up with too much too long, and now I'm just too intelligent, too powerful, too beautiful, too sure of who I am finally to deserve anything less."

Edual, 23 years old.

I HAVE ALWAYS BEEN QUEER SINCE THE SECOND I WAS BORN. IT JUST TOOK ME A WHILE TO REALIZE IT, THEN TO ACCEPT IT.

I WAS THE BIGGEST TOMBOY AROUND PLAYING JUST AS ROUGH AND TOUGH AS ANY BOY, IN fact even better. It was natural. I knew no other way. No Barbies for me! No Way! He Man and G.I. Joe were the order of the day. If you could get me to stand still long enough to play house, I had to be the son or the father. At one point, I think I even thought I was a boy and became very disappointed upon learning that I wasn't.

It is definitely a credit to my family and friends that I was never told my behavior was wrong or weird. One incident comes to mind when I made my feelings for one of my sister's friends apparent. I must have been eight or ten at the time. She was at least four years older. The revelation really grossed her out and she stormed out of the room. My sister ran after her and defended my actions by saying, "She's like that" and "that's the way she is; she doesn't mean anything." But, oh did I. I suppose that's why when I finally did come out to my mom and sister eight years later, it wasn't much of a surprise. I guess deep down they've always known or suspected that I was queer. They just needed to hear it from me.

Whether you believe queerness is inherent or acquired I don't think it really matters. I knew who I was even at a young age. My childhood was riddled with the usual stories about experimenting sexually. To no one's surprise my adolescence was no picnic. Whoever said "growing up is hard to do" was definitely watering things down. I developed crushes on most of the women that crossed my way via televi-sion, film, and videos. Oh, videos. I think I had a crush on every reinvention of Madonna's look. From her original Boy Toy image to Truth or Dare to the present baby boom. The crushes and feelings were always there, I just didn't have the vocabulary to describe exactly what they were.

School wasn't as bad as some stories I've heard. At least there was one advocate there dropping hints when discussions would break out in class. She always seemed to direct them at me and I resented her for that at the time. When it finally dawned on me that I was queer, I denied it to myself, and that hurt the most. I've never questioned the suicide statistics, I've been there.

I could go on and on about the alienation and iso-lation of not only adolescence but "queer adoles-cence." I feared the road ahead of me because of my proverbial "preconditioned destiny." A minority, a woman, and queer! Who could ask for anything more?

No matter how bleak things seemed, I realized they could be a lot worse. Once I got over my initial denial and then fear, I eventually learned that I love who I am and wouldn't have it any other way. My queerness, my differences, my experiences, they make me who I am today. And me alone. The gen-uine article.

I'm here sharing my story so that others can bene-fit and learn from it. To deny it would be a shame; to vanish it would be criminal.

Being out isn't a static sole event where you do it once and you never have to do it again it's a constant. I've been out for 4 years but in my everyday existance I don't feel like I need to out myself every waking hour -- that would be quite exhausting. I'm just myself (whatever that means), unwilling to hide, though I don't wear "freedom rings" or pink/black triangles. I just am.

Salva 22

RAFAEL

○

I STARTED HAVING SEXUAL FEELINGS TOWARD MEN WHEN I WAS FOURTEEN. I REMEMBER BEING SCARED, BECAUSE I DIDN'T KNOW ANYONE WHO HAD THE SAME FEELINGS. BECAUSE I WAS BROUGHT UP IN A VERY STRICT CATHOLIC HOME, I THOUGHT THAT SOMETHING WAS WRONG with me. By the time I was sixteen I knew I was gay. I was lonely and unhappy for a long time. I wanted to tell people: my best friend, my mom, my dad, everyone, but I was scared that they wouldn't understand. Finally I did tell my best friend and to my surprise he was cool with it. That gave me a new hope that not everyone hated gays.

I was asked to leave home shortly after I came out, not only because of my sexual orientation, but also because of other things that were going on at that time. I moved to Boston and let the street show me what it meant to be gay. I thank God that I had a boyfriend who took me in and let me live with him. He gave me a new life. He told me that being gay was no different from being straight. You see, I thought that people had to change everything just because they were gay. I actually thought that I needed to act, dress, and look different because I was gay.

Being young and gay in a new town was incredibly difficult. I knew no one except my boyfriend and his friends. The only friends I had of my own were prostitutes. I didn't know where to meet other gay youth. You see, straight kids can go anywhere and meet one another. They also don't get hassled when they express affection in public. When I was young the only real place to meet someone for a relationship was in a bar. I had to sneak into bars between the ages of seventeen and twenty-one. Needless to say, I started drinking and drugging at a young age. Now I know what you are saying is that young kids, gay or straight, will drink or drug. This is true, but gay, lesbian, bisexual, and transgender youth have no place to go except to a bar to meet someone, so the chances of one of them becoming an alcoholic are much greater than that of a straight kid.

By the grace of God everything has worked itself out. My parents and I have a better relationship now than ever before. I have found my pride, strength, and dignity. I have a great job doing what I like, educating and breaking stereotypes in order to make a better world.

As a gay young adult, I feel there is only one person you need to come out to and that is yourself. I think young adults have a responsibility to make themselves visible, but only if and when they feel safe. If you decide to come out to your parents, give them time. Remember how long it took you to accept yourself. Give your parents twice as long to get over their misconceptions.

Raff 22 yrs. old.

DANIELLE

◐

I CAME OUT TO MY FRIENDS AT FIFTEEN AND TO MY FAMILY SOON AFTER THAT. I KNEW I HAD TO TELL MY PARENTS BEFORE SOMEONE ELSE DID. TELLING MY MOM WAS PERHAPS THE MOST STRESSFUL TIME OF MY LIFE. I HAD NO IDEA HOW SHE WAS GOING TO REACT. I ENDED UP CRY-

ing out of nervousness before I even told her. She ended up crying as well, but not out of disappointment or anger. It was out of concern for my well-being and my future. She knew I would have a long road ahead and she wished it didn't have to be so hard. She ended up telling my dad for me and that was all right as well. In fact it was excellent. After that I had a great feeling of relief. My siblings have been wonderful, too. As a matter of fact, my brother wrote me a letter saying how proud he was of me for coming out and that he still loved me the same. Knowing my brother I know that it wasn't easy for him to express himself like that. I really treasure that letter. Knowing that I could go home to people who cared and that I could release all my rage to them was so uplifting. I didn't have to lie to my family or friends anymore. I could actually feel a great weight

being lifted off my shoulders. I felt free and it was wonderful.

I had a hard time coming out in my high school. I was harassed there with lots of name-calling, threats, and being pushed around in the hallways. They even gave my friends a hard time. It was very emotionally trying. But junior year some students who knew what I had gone through approached me and asked me to start a gay/straight alliance because they were too scared to do it themselves. I spent two years working very hard to start a GSA and by the time I graduated, it was quite the successful group. Through other organizations I started to speak publicly about my experiences coming out and what life was like for me.

That brings me to now. I am about to start my life as a college student in the fall and I'm looking forward to moving on to new things.

I can remember as a little kid being different than the other little girls. I didn't want to wear dresses and play with dolls, but I knew even then that it went beyond that. I knew I was different inside, but I didn't know how. I can remember around nine or ten feeling so completely isolated and confused that I wanted to end my life. I was being ostracized and felt like a complete and total freak. Most of the kids would have nothing to do with me. I was ridiculed and called Tomboy. By the time I was twelve or thirteen I had a term for myself, something I could categorize myself as, and that was gay. I could finally understand why I couldn't look at a boy as 'cute' but could see a girl as beautiful.

Danielle 17

WILLIAM

◐

ITHINK I CAME OUT AT FIRST BECAUSE I WAS HORNY.

YES, I WAS DEPRESSED, LONELY, ISOLATED, AND SCARED, TOO. BUT AT EIGHTEEN YEARS OLD I THINK THE FEELINGS THAT WERE AT THE FOREFRONT WERE ABOUT SEX. I WAS A BOY BRIM-

ming with desire with no proper way or skills to express it, name it, or even really understand it. Where was a boy to go when he had so many questions in need of being researched? The library.

So I went to the library and read.

I read Edmund White, Bret Easton Ellis, George Whitmore, James Baldwin. I read them all for the sex. Skipping through the books for the scandalous parts. Scenes of men touching, kissing, making love. I was in heaven.

But while I was looking for one thing, I found another: a series of experiences, a set of emotions that echoed my own, beyond sexual desire. I found characters who were lonely like I was, sad like I was, and some characters who were happy living lives I was not even sure were possible. Lives in New York, Paris, even Ohio. They were all gay, all fabulous. I hit pay dirt. I got hope (and some saucy tales to boot).

Those written words showed me a community.

And in the end that community helped me take my first step in coming out.

My first coming out was like a Sleeping Beauty wake-up call. It felt like a dream that previously I could not wake up from had finally ended.

I was so happy.

The curse lifted.

A whole set of wondrous, scary, unknown possibilities lay in front of me. Of course I had told only my freshman English teacher, who was moving to Europe and whom I would never see again, after the last day of class. But hell, it was a start. And I knew it would lead me to tell my best friend, my parents, my classmates. I knew then, as I know now, that the truth is a great thing. Once you speak it and let it go, it will run its course and soon turn up everywhere.

The spark had been lit, and next came the fire. I could hardly wait.

Here are some favorite questions from people who are afraid of us: Why Do you have to flaunt it!? Why do you have to be so vocal!? Here are some answers (from a person who is vocal and who does flaunt it): I get called faggot on the street by people who hate me but don't even know me. Many people want to die because the world says being gay is wrong. Kissing a boy can get you killed. In schools around the country children are not safe. It's not a crime to like show tunes, have a great fashion sense and dance to disco. Lastly, IF I do not define my oppression and fight it, I have an aching feeling my oppression will not only define me but if it has it's way, destroy me.

— William 22

LYNN

◐

DISCOVERING MY TRUE SEXUAL IDENTITY DIDN'T JUST HAPPEN ONE DAY LIKE AN EPIPHANY. IT WAS MORE A SERIES OF QUESTIONS AND FEELINGS THAT I BEGAN TO RECOGNIZE. RETROSPECTIVELY, I CAN REMEMBER CERTAIN THINGS THAT WOULD NOW BE clues, like my friend who made me feel "fluttery" inside when we would play, or the foreign exchange student who came to stay once, and I wondered what it would be like to kiss her.

My family moved when I was in high school and I met two women who became very important people to me. As my understanding of their relationship grew, questions of my own identity began to surface. I decided that my questions were merely the result of many enlightened conversations with the two of them. It wasn't until I went away to college that I realized I might be wrong.

I was a college freshman when I kissed my first girl. Wow! That kiss made everything fall into place. Finally I understood all the feelings that I had been feeling, and all the questions I had been asking.

My close friends at the time were an extremely supportive group and I am convinced that this made all the difference in my feeling comfortable enough to come out. All of them were wonderful, listening to me ramble on about my confusion and supporting all of my choices. When I moved across the country, I met the person who is now my best friend. She came to be the strength I had left behind when I moved.

I came out to my family about four years after I first came out to myself. The news was not well received at first, and my relationship with my mother took quite a beating for a while. We've come a long way and talk as adults now. We've both apologized for things said and done.

When I think about those who I admire, celebrities don't come to mind. I hold great respect for ordinary people who come out in the workplace, the neighborhood, and in their families. People who are out and proud every day of their lives, because they believe in themselves. These are the people who inspire me. I know how hard it can be. I do it myself.

I still have the same joys and frustrations with relationships that straight people do, but for me the joys are that much greater because they are visible expressions of my true feelings. I still haven't found Ms. Right. (Of course there is the recurring fantasy of Melissa Ethridge dumping Julie and marrying me.) At any rate, I'm not worried. I'm young and I have my whole life ahead of me.

"You don't look like a lesbian", a guy said to me recently. First off, for the sake of labels, I identify as a bisexual. His comment, though carelessly spoken, made me stop and think. What exactly does a lesbian look like? or a bisexual for that matter? As far as this guy was concerned, I simply could not be gay because I didn't fit his image or society's image of what a lesbian looks like. But that's the point. I'm an individual, unique in many different ways. I don't fit a stereotype because I'm a real person. My sexual orientation is just another page in the story that makes up my life.

Lynn Age 21

NATHAN

◐

I MAGINE I'M TWENTY-ONE YEARS OLD AND I AM ASKING "WHO AM I?" WASN'T I SUPPOSED TO DO THAT WHEN I WAS THIRTEEN? SHOULDN'T THIS HAVE BEEN DONE ALREADY? BUT REALLY, WHEN I THINK ABOUT IT, I HAVE SPENT SO MUCH TIME LYING AND HIDING, NO WONDER I'M SO confused. So now I've opened up this box of fear and simply accepted it. I've folded up all my Sundays spent in church crying inside, flattened out all the confusion felt on all sides—family, friends, and self. Most of all I released all the fear I had of the world outside, the ignorance, and hate. I tucked it back and pushed it in the corner of the barn or attic, I forget now, and just let it go. Now what I am left with: a family album, an old pair of torn jeans, my favorite sweater, and me. Someone sure to be true to myself, kind, strong, and happy.

Now I am free, I can move my body in all directions and feel my muscles tense and relax, to create the movements that express what I truly feel. I have not always felt this way.

My church said I was going to burn in hell. My family would crack fag jokes and talk about gays as if they were some kind of perverse clowns. I thought I was the only one in the world to feel so trapped and worthless. I was positive that I was the only one to walk through the woods talking to the trees, thinking they would keep my secrets. I could hear them at night crying as the wind taunted them to tell. Then I would sleep and in my sleep I would be dancing, always moving to reach the place deep inside where my emotions were held. The things I kept secret in the day became my dreams at night—my walks through the woods, a secret money can for when I made my escape, a crush on the man who worked at the stables down the road, and my love of movement which no one seemed to understand.

I saw dance like a secret language, every person having his own "motion dialect," each motion meaning something the soul wants to say. My movements were my mark, my pink triangle being my thin limbs and graceful ways. My parents couldn't understand why I would not play a sport, and my peers teased me endlessly, so I quit at fifteen. I turned my body into a cage, that way no one could chalk a triangle on me or make me cry with their words. So I learned to fake it for a while and made it through high school with only a couple of scars. In college I learned how foolish I was to give people power over me that they really did not have. That power belonged to me all along, not them. I came out to my friends and soon felt the strength to dance again. I laugh and smile. My body no longer being a cage, I can love whomever I choose. I am free. I can breathe.

If anyone wants to know what it feels like to be in
the closet
find a deep, empty well, jump down to the bottom, and sit there.

Wait a day...   ... and a night...
                    ... and the next day...

never knowing if you'll move in a wide open space again.
Nathan 21

ANDY

○

HIGH SCHOOL WAS A GREAT EXPERIENCE FOR ME ACADEMICALLY, BUT WHEN YOU TALK ABOUT MY PERSONAL NEEDS, SUCH AS BEING PART OF A GROUP, YOU COULD SAY THE GATE TO THE PARK WAS ALWAYS CLOSED.

For the first three years of high school, the closet was my home. I lived in the Dominican Republic, which is an extremely antigay country. Being gay there was not an easy thing to deal with because of what was expected of me culturally and socially. I moved back to the States for my senior year, where I had attended grammar and elementary school. I returned to gain information about college and to make changes in my personal life.

In the States I found my place in high school. I realized that I was not alone in this world and that there were others who cared. They helped me see myself as a student, as a professional, and, most important, as a gay Hispanic male.

The best kind of support that teachers, peers, and friends can offer me and others is to be educated and knowledgeable about gay issues and about the problems gay youth face dealing with everyday life. They can simply let us know that they are there for us with the respect and understanding that we need. They do not need to give us special treatment but just to treat us the same as others.

For me as a gay Latino man, expressing who I love is very important, because I am being myself. For the me to say "I love this man" is like saying I love my freedom.

In order for you to know all of me you must know that I am:

- Gay — Simple
- Latino — Understanding
- Proud — and most of all Human.

P.S. I have a complete and total crush on Chris O'Donnell

Andy   age 19

ATIENO

◑

I HAVE NEVER REALLY HAD TO HIDE WITH MY FAMILY. WE ARE A PRETTY OPEN AND HONEST GROUP OF FOLKS AND TRY HARD NOT TO MAKE VALUE JUDGMENTS. THE ONLY ONE I DIDN'T SHARE MY SEXUAL PREFERENCE WITH WAS MY BROTHER, WHO IS NOW DECEASED, BECAUSE HE

was *really* homophobic. As an African American, I think folks of color still seem to have a bigger problem with lesbians and gays and they will dog you if you give them a chance. You really have to choose your friends carefully, and proceed with caution until you really know a person.

I live in a city where tolerance is expected and intolerance is frowned upon. The high school I attended is very progressive. It wasn't very hard for me there. I didn't advertise but I didn't have to feel embarrassed. Some kids are still kind of skittish about sex and sexuality.

This is America where everyone is supposed to be free. When you think about it, we are all visitors in this country. This land belonged to the Native Americans. Everyone else is an immigrant. I say this because everyone should have an opportunity to be whatever and whoever she or he wants to be. No one has the right to deny or censor anyone else. I'm not saying "get in your face," but if I'm gay and proud, then that is my prerogative. We are who we are and we can't be anything else. I believe this African proverb sums it up: "Rain beats a leopard's skin, but it does not wash out the spots."

A year ago my brother was killed and I realized
that life was too short to not be myself. So I
decided to come out.

Atieno 19

ROBERT

◐

A day in my life:

Damn, the alarm clock is ringing. Where is that snooze button?

Good, silence . . .

Damn, the alarm clock is ringing, again. I better get up or I'll be late for school. That's just what I need, detention for being late. Now if I can only find that room with the thing that drops water on you . . . what's it called? Oh . . . bathroom!

Well, I am awake now. Let's see, I can brush my hair and eat breakfast in the car. Okay, let's go.

Okay, at school, with five minutes to spare . . . bonus!

There's Darren. He's kinda cute, but he's too full of himself. I guess that's what happens when you're the football star and can have any girl in school.

Oh no, Melissa. Quick, duck into the band room. I can't face her now. I like her and all, but only as a friend. I don't know how to tell her. Maybe I should say yes, I mean, I've never had a real girlfriend and I am seventeen. All of my friends are dating someone. I guess I'm kinda unusual. I'm just not interested in girls. I've tried, believe me. I tried to understand what I should like about girls when Dave and I talked.

I tried to be a "normal" guy with Mary, but it just felt weird. It was as though I was forcing myself to say those words, or to hold her. I figured that if I did, the feelings would grow, but they never did. So now I have Melissa wanting to put me in that position and I know I would rather spend a weekend with Grandma than that. I have to tell Melissa no. Maybe the feelings didn't come because Mary and I never went on a date. I don't know.

Good, she didn't even notice me. Now to get to class.

I love calculus. I wonder what my teacher is babbling about today. Oh, there's Steve. Now he's gorgeous. I heard that he and Stephanie broke up. I would really like to get to know him better. He seems really cool. What? Did he say a calculus test? I'll have to ask Kerry later if that's true.

I wouldn't ever say anything to Steve. I'm too scared, besides he wouldn't want to be friends with me, I'm just a nerd.

Great. Class is over. Maybe I'll get a glimpse of Steve before lunch if I'm lucky, 'cause the sights get barren for the rest of the day.

Maybe I'm gay. No, I'm not. I'm just not interested in girls yet, it will happen when I get a little older. But how old? I mean, I'm already seventeen and it should have hit me by now. If I was gay I would have to be attracted to guys. I think Steve is nice and all, but I don't want to do anything with him. Besides, I don't want to wear a dress or parade down Broadway wearing a thong bikini. I can't be gay.

. . . I gave in to what I was feeling. I said, "I'm gay." To hear those words come out of my mouth was the best thing. I accepted who I was and what I am. I realized that I can't choose who I am attracted to.

I came out to end the pain. Denying who I am was the worst form of torture in the world. I thought if I came out I would loose my parents, friends, basically everyone I knew. For months, I constantly thought of suicide. I figured I wasn't worthy of being alive, because I was attracted to members of my sex. The hiding almost destroyed me.

Now everyone knows my secret and I'm still alive. I have all the friends I had before the "bombshell", plus many more because of being gay. All my friends stayed and my parents didn't cut me off. Now I can be myself around everyone I know. The world I came out to was better than my wildest dreams.

Robert
Age: 20

LIZ

◐

I was called a dyke before I knew what the word meant or that I was one. I was fourteen at summer camp when I looked at the wall above my best friend's bed and saw written there "Liz is a dyke." I walked over to the other girls who were shav-ing their legs and said, trying to restrain my anger, "I have no idea who wrote this, but I am so offended. I'm not a dyke and I am really sick of people making fun of me." I saw them exchange looks and run their eyes up my unshaven legs before they turned away from me and fastened the attention back on their foamy legs. I walked to my friend's bed, sat down, and turned to her. "What's a dyke?"

"A lesbian," she said.

I looked at her and said, "I'm not, you know."

So I knew that lesbian was something to be avoided instinctively, automatically. I wrote in my journal that summer, "Something that really bugs me is the way people treat the idea of lesbianism— it's like a big joke. 'Listen,' I feel like saying, 'they aren't the same as you. But that doesn't make them bad or wrong.'"

Eight months later I figured out the truth of the matter. It seems that the writing on the wall is always some kind of portent. I was lucky in every sense. I spent dozens of long afternoons in the library between the high stacks that dwarfed me, pulling down one book after another on gay life, lesbian history, Stonewall, politics. I found the most hidden corners of the library, the carrels that fit in the corner so no one could see the reader. I even tucked my legs beneath me so nobody could identify my sneakers as I absorbed my culture through the dog-eared pages. When it came time for my parents to pick me up, I went to the feminist section and brought home a hefty stack: *The Second Sex, Gyn/Ecology, Of Woman Born, Sexual Politics.*

I assumed that feminism was a code word for lesbian. I must have reread Simone de Beauvoir's chapter "The Lesbian" seven times. At fourteen I made the mistake of taking for truth everything the books said. That I made the assumption that all feminists were embracing of the lesbian experience was to be expected. Today, when I read de Beauvoir's chapter "The Lesbian," I am struck by the crude stereotypes and the Freudian tenets. Five years ago I was much too happy even to see the word in print to object.

From feminist texts, I started to explore literature. The first book I remember reading with any lesbian content was Lillian Hellman's *The Children's Hour*. I read that play *underneath* the desks of the carrels at school. I cried when I finished reading, not because the lesbian character killed herself but because there was a character who acknowledged the fact that she was drawn to other women. I loved that play. I read it once a week. By the end of the year I could manage to read it sitting at a desk even though I flipped to *The Little Foxes* every time someone I knew approached.

I hid, often, in the library and between the stacks, when I knew I was alone. I whispered, "I'm gay. I'm gay." Even if it was only to tell the characters in the books, even if those characters in the books lifted shotguns to their heart, I needed them to know. I moved aside the books, and on the corner of the oak bookshelf in a shaky hand, penciled "I'm gay." I rubbed my sweaty fingers over the words until they smeared into a fine dust. I knew the words had existed. I knew the dust would stay.

You can put a label on me — call me a big dyke, call me damned,
call me whatever you want — and you will not come close to the truth
of what I am. I'm a woman, I'm a poet, I'm a daughter, a sister, a
friend. I'm an activist, I'm a Jew, I'm a leader, a scholar, a fighter.
I'm a lesbian. I am not afraid. And I am happy.

                                                    —Liz, 18

The following list of resources is a starting point from which to find information and materials on lesbian, gay, and bisexual issues. This list represents only a fraction of the resources available to lesbian, gay, and bisexual young people, and their families, teachers, and friends. There is a vast network of resources and support out here for you. Take heart, you are not alone.

BOOKS AND PAMPHLETS

YOUTH

Bass, Ellen, and Kate, Kaufman. *Free Your Mind: The Book for Gay, Lesbian, and Bisexual Youth— and Their Allies.* New York: HarperPerennial, 1996.

Bauer, Marion Dane, ed. *Am I Blue: Coming Out from the Silence.* HarperCollins, 1994.

Borhek, Mary V. *Coming Out to Parents: A Two-way Survival Guide for Lesbians and Gay Men and Their Parents.* Cleveland, OH: Pilgrim Press, 1993.

Chandler, Kurt. *Passages of Pride: Lesbian and Gay Youth Come of Age.* New York: Random House, 1995.

Cranston, Kevin, and Cooper Thompson. *I Think I Might Be Gay . . . Now What Do I Do?* Cambridge, MA: The Campaign to End Homophobia, 1989, 1993. (617-868-8280)

Eichberg, Rob. *Coming Out: An Act of Love.* New York: Dutton, 1990.

Federation of Parents, Friends, and Families of Lesbians and Gays (PFLAG). *Be Yourself: Questions and Answers for Gay, Lesbian and Bisexual Youth.* Washington, DC: PFLAG, 1994. (202-638-4200; fax: (202-638-0243)

Heron, Ann, ed. *Two Teenagers in Twenty: Writings by Gay and Lesbian Youth.* Boston: Alyson Publications, Inc., 1994. (800-5-ALYSON)

Hutchins, Loraine, and Lani Kaahumanu, eds. *Bi Any Other Name: Bisexual People Speak Out.* Boston: Alyson Publications, Inc., 1991. (800-5-ALYSON)

Luzak, Raymond. *Eyes of Desire.* Boston: Alyson Publications, Inc., 1993. (Deaf lesbians and gays tell their stories.) (800-5-ALYSON)

Marcus, Eric. *Is It a Choice?: Answers to 300 of the Most Frequently Asked Questions About Gays and Lesbians.* San Francisco: HarperSanFrancisco, 1993.

Members of OUTRIGHT et al. *I Think I Might Be a Lesbian . . . Now What Do I Do?* Cambridge, MA: The Campaign to End Homophobia. (617-868-8280)

National Youth Advocacy Coalition. *Improving the Lives of Gay, Lesbian, Bisexual and Transgender Youth.* 1711 Connecticut Avenue, NW, Suite 206, Washington, DC 20009; (202-319-7596; fax: 202-319-7365; E-mail: nyouthac@aol.com.)

The Shared Heart Initiatives, *The Shared Heart Initiatives Resource Guide.* P.O. Box 562, Brookline, MA 02146; (617-536-7050, ext. 27.)

Singer, Bennett L., ed. *Growing Up Gay: A Literary Anthology.* New York: The New Press, 1993.

PARENTS/FAMILIES

Aarons, Leroy. *Prayers for Bobby: A Mother's Coming to Terms with the Suicide of Her Gay Son.* San Francisco: HarperSanFrancisco, 1995.

Bernstein, Robert A. *Straight Parents/Gay Children: Keeping Families Together.* Thunder's Mouth Press, 1995.

Dew, Robb Forman. *The Family Heart: A Memoir of When Our Son Came Out.* New York: Ballantine, 1995.

Fairchild, Betty, and Nancy Harward. *Now That You Know: What Every Parent Should Know About Homosexuality.* New York: Harvest Books, 1989.

Martin, April. *The Lesbian and Gay Parenting Handbook: Creating and Raising Our Families.* New York: HarperCollins, 1993.

Sexuality Information and Education Council of the United States (SEICUS). *How to Talk to Your Children About AIDS.* New York: SEICUS, 1994. (212-819-9770).

TEACHERS/STUDENTS

Berzon, Betty. *Setting Them Straight: You Can Do Something About Bigotry and Homophobia.* New York: Penguin Books, 1996. (212-645-3121)

National Youth Advocacy Coalition, Bridges Project. *Education Issues Information Packet: Addressing Sexual Orientation and Developing Support Systems in Schools.* 1711 Connecticut Avenue, NW, Suite 206, Washington, DC 20009; 202-319-7596; fax: 202-319-7365; E-mail: nyouthac@aol.com.

————. *Safe Zone Campaign.* 1711 Connecticut Avenue, NW, Suite 206, Washington, DC 20009; 202-319-7596; fax: 202-319-7365; E-mail: nyouthac@aol.com.

Norcio, Diane et al., eds. *Open Communities, Open Minds: Peer Leadership Promoting Safety for Gay, Lesbian, and Bisexual Youth.* Boston: Prevention Support Services, 1995. Massachusetts Department of Public Health. The Medical Foundation, 95 Berkeley Street, Boston, MA 02116; 617-451-0049.

P.E.R.S.O.N. Project, The. *The P.E.R.S.O.N. Organizing Manual: Public Education Regarding Sexual Orientation Nationally.* E-mail: richter@eecs.berkeley.edu;web: http://www.youth.org/loco/PERSONProject/.

Phariss, Tracy. *A Bibliography: Lesbian, Gay and Bisexual Issues in Education* (1996). GLSTN Colorado, P.O. Box 280346, Lakewood, CO 80228; 303-936-6562; E-mail: glstnco@aol.com.

Safe Schools Coalition of Washington. *Safe Schools Anti Violence Documentation Project Annual Report.* The Northwest Coalition Against Malicious Harassment, P.O. Box 16776, Seattle WA 98116; 206-233-9136; web:http://members. tripod.com/~claytoly/safe.

Safe Schools Program for Gay and Lesbian Students. *Gay/Straight Alliances: A Student Guide.* Massachusetts Department of Education, 350 Main Street, Malden, MA 02148-5023; 617-388-3300, Ext.389.

Williams, Richard, Worldwide Manager, AIDS Awareness Program. *When A Co-Worker Is Living with AIDS: A Guide for the Workplace.* Polaroid Corporation, 565 Technology Square, 7, Cambridge, MA 02139; 617-386-3879.

NATIONAL HOT LINES

Linea Nacional de SIDA. 800-344-7432. Daily.

Massachusetts Gay and Lesbian Youth Peer Listening Line. 800-399-PEER, Monday to Friday 4 P.M.–10 P.M. Nationwide calls welcome.

National AIDS Hot Line. 800-342-AIDS or 800-AIDS-TTY, 24-hour service.

National Runaway Switchboard. 800-621-4000, 7 days a week, 24 hours a day. Hot line for runaway/homeless youth and their families.

Out Youth Austin Help Line. 800-96-Youth, daily 5:30 P.M.–9:30 P.M. CST. Nationwide calls welcome. Peer support and resources for gay, lesbian, bisexual, and questioning youth.

Samariteens. 800-252-TEEN, 7 days a week 2 P.M.–11 P.M. Peer-run suicide prevention hot line.

NATIONAL RESOURCE ORGANIZATIONS

YOUTH

Alcoholics Anonymous, P.O. Box 459, Grand Central Station, New York, NY 10163; (general service office) 212-870-3400; fax: 212-870-3003, web: http//www. ALCOHOLICS-ANONYMOUS.org.

National AIDS Information Clearinghouse, P.O. Box 6003, Rockville, MD 20849-6003; 800-458-5231; fax: 301-251-5343 web: http://www.cdc-nac.org.

Rainbow Alliance of the Deaf, P.O. Box 14182, Washington, DC 20044-4128.

PARENTS/FAMILIES

Parents, Families, and Friends of Lesbians and Gays (PFLAG), 1101 14th Street NW, Washington, DC 20005; 202-638-4200; fax: 202-638-0243; E-mail: pflagntl@aol.com. Call for a list of PFLAG groups and information nationwide.

American Civil Liberties Union (ACLU), National Gay and Lesbian Rights Project, 132 West 43rd Street, New York, NY 10036; 212-944-9800, ext. 545; fax: 212-869-9065; web:www.aclu.org.

American Friends Services Committee, Pacific Northwest Regional Office Safe Schools Coalition, 814 N.E. 40th Street, Seattle, WA 98105; 206-632-0500; fax: 206-632-0976; web: afsc.org.

Gay, Lesbian, and Straight Teachers Network (GLSTN), 122 West 26th Street, Suite 1100, New York, NY 10001; 212-727-0135; E-mail: glstn@glstn.org;web:http://www.glstn. org. /respect.

National Education Association Gay and Lesbian Caucus, P.O. Box 3559, York, PA 17402; 717-848-3354; fax: 717-843-9790; web: jtesterman@aol.com.

GUIDES TO LOCAL ORGANIZATIONS

To locate gay, lesbian, and bisexual youth resource organizations in your area:

Lambda Youth Network, P.O. Box 7911, Culver City, CA 90233; E-mail: lambdayn@aol.com.

National Youth Advocacy Coalition, Bridges Project, 1711 Connecticut Avenue, NW, Suite 206, Washington, DC 20009; 202-319-7596; fax: 202-319-7365; E-mail: nyouthac@aol.com.

SPIRITUALITY RESOURCE ORGANIZATIONS

These organizations can help you find groups in your area.

Baptist: American Baptists Concerned, P.O. Box 16128, Oakland, CA 94610; 510-530-6562; fax: 510-530-6501; E-mail: ambaptists@aol.com.

Buddhist: The San Francisco Zen Center, 300 Page Street, San Francisco, CA 94102; 415-863-3136; fax: 415-431-9220; E-mail: sf zen@postoffice. pacbell.net.

Episcopal: Integrity, Inc., P.O. Box 5255, New York, NY 10185-5255; phone and fax: 908-220-1914; E-mail markk8@interserv.com; web: http//members.aol. com./natlinteg/.

Evangelical: Evangelicals Concerned, 311 E. 72nd Street, Suite 1-G, New York, NY 10021; 212-517-3171.

Jewish: World Congress of Gay and Lesbian Jewish Organizations, P.O. Box 3345, New York, NY 10008-3345.

MCC: Universal Fellowship of Metropolitan Community Churches, 8704 Santa Monica Boulevard, 2nd floor, West Hollywood, CA 90069; 310-360-8640; fax: 310-360-8680; E-mail: ufmcchq@aol.com.

Mormon: Affirmation, P.O. Box 46022, Los Angeles, CA 90046; 213-255-7251; E-mail: http://ng.netgate.net/ jfirth/affirmation.

Presbyterian: Presbyterians for Lesbian/Gay Concerns, P.O. Box 38, New Brunswick, NJ 08903-0038; 908-249-1016; fax: 908-932-6916; E-mail: jda@mariner. rutgers.edu.

Quaker: Friends for Lesbian and Gay Concerns, 143 Campbell Avenue, Ithaca, NY 14850; 607-272-1024; fax: 607-272-0801.

Roman Catholic: Dignity/USA, 1500 Massachusetts Avenue, NW, Suite 11, Washington, DC 20005; 202-861-0017 or 800-877-8797; fax: 202-429-9808.

Unitarian Universalist: Unitarian Universalist Office of Lesbian, Bisexual, Gay & Transgendered Concerns, 25 Beacon Street, Boston, MA 02108; 617-742-2100, x 470; fax: 617-367-3237; E-mail: bgreve@uua.org.

The young people who participated in this project are the driving force behind its creation. It is because of their strength and courage that this book exists. Their unyielding commitment to be themselves is the foundation of this work. I am privileged to know each of them and am grateful that they welcomed me into their lives.

This book and the touring exhibit of photographs created from it were nurtured and developed by an extraordinary group of talented and committed people, the Board of Directors of The Shared Heart, Inc. It has been my great opportunity to work with and learn from each of them. Michael Ward, our President, is a dynamic leader and a cohesive force. His commitment to service and huge heart guide our work. He is a great friend to all of us and especially to me. Our Vice President, Liz Page, brings impeccable style, direction, and expertise to our board. Liz takes a passionate stand for human beings and works with a curious mind and a grateful heart. David Latham, our treasurer, contributes wisdom and guidance. David's clarity and integrity direct the board with steady skillfulness. Tim Collins is the visionary who saw the potential for this work and opened doors to facilitate its creation. Reverend Kim K. Crawford Harvie brings great insight, humor, compassion, and spiritual guidance. She is a community leader with an unfailing commitment to young people. Paul Davis Jones's creativity and imagination help us to see the bigger picture and actualize what is possible. I am grateful to Ram Dass for recognizing the importance of The Shared Heart and offering his endorsement. Rick Williams, our quintessential educator, brings his profound understanding of diversity, development and the educational potential of the arts to this project. Rick possesses a tireless commitment to social justice and the creation of an equitable world. Each of these remarkable individuals has given enormous amounts of time, energy, and love to this project. I am grateful to them all. Special thanks to the members of the Shared Heart Advisory Board: Ann Gifford, Joan Parker, and Ellen Payzant.

The Shared Heart was made possible through the visionary leadership and generosity of BankBoston and the Threshold Foundation.

Major gifts from the following individuals and organizations helped to transform this work from a possibility into a reality. Arlington Street Church, John H. Basile, Emanuel Berger, Boston Lesbian and Gay Communities Funding Partnership at the Boston Foundation, John Brewer, Desmond Child, Citizens Bank of Massachusetts, Harry Collings Achievement Endowment, Tim Collins, Concord Academy, Sheila D'Alessandro & Heather Smith, Thomas Decker, Arthur Dion & Gallery Naga, Michael Dively, Emory University, Forest Foundation, Gay Rights Grass Roots Fund, Arlene Fortunato, Anne & Chad Gifford, Burton Goldstein, Groton School, Robert Hardman, IBM, Martha & Ira Jackson, Paul Davis Jones, Myra & Robert Kraft, Kripalu Center, David J. Latham, Thomas A. Leavitt & Arcadia Press, Peter Lubin, David Murphy & Stanhope Framers, Joan & Robert Parker, Phillips Academy, Polaroid Foundation, Lee Ridgeway & Donald Vaughan, Dr. Richard Saul, Howard Siegel, Spirit Rock Wednesday AM Meditation Group, James Stone & Monrüd, The Cellar Door Companies, The David Geffen Foundation, The Tides Foundation, The Tiger Fund of The Unitarian Universalist Urban Ministry, Victory Programs, Inc., Ellen & Daniel Weiner, Richard Williams, and Walter Yetnikoff.

The following individuals and organizations have generously given their time, expertise, and resources to facilitate the successful completion of this project. John Affuso, Jack Armitage, Paul Astwood, Sylvia Boorstein, Eric Boroush, Sharon Brash, Candler Creative, Ken Carl, Jonathan Cleveland, Nina Dawe, Doreen A. DuCom, Pamela Duffy, Kate & Joel Feldman, Anne & Chad Gifford, Richard Giglio, Gwen Gordon, Ken Allen Hadden, Steven Holt, Ira Jackson, Leslie A. Joseph, Toni Kenny, Ron King, Michael Kozuch, Latham and Latham P. C., Kent Lew, Nina Markham, Jed Mattes, Bridget McGuiness, Harriet Meikeljohn, Maurice Melchiono, Peter Hamilton Nee, Karen Newkirk, Rasmani Orth, Liz Page Associates, Joan Parker, Ellen Payzant, Julie Rhoad, Cathy Roth, Daniel Salera, Maureen A. Sheehan, Peter Taussig, The Gay and Lesbian Visitors Center at the 1996

Centenial Olympics, The IDPR Group, Brian Vail, David Vigliano, A. J. Wasson and Kim Westheimer.

The following individuals and organizations graciously offered their names in support of this project. They are allies for a safe and healthy world for all young people: Michael Duffy, Chairman, Massachusetts Commission Against Discrimination; Scott Harshbarger, Attorney General, The Commonwealth of Massachusetts Office of the Attorney General; Nancy Jackson, Executive Co-Director, New England Consortium for Families and Youth; Jeff Perrotti, Director, The Commonwealth of Massachusetts Department of Education Safe Schools Program for Gay and Lesbian Students; David LaFontaine & Edward LeMay, The Massachusetts Governor's Commission on Gay and Lesbian Youth; Thomas M. Menino, Mayor, City of Boston, Massachusetts; Thomas W. Payzant, Superintendent, Boston Public Schools; PFLAG: Parents, Families and Friends of Lesbians and Gays; The Lesbian & Gay Political Alliance of Massachusetts.

I thank my dear family for their encouragement and love. I am grateful to my mom, Dr. Herma Mastoon, for her absolute support and belief in me, and for teaching me that everything is possible; my dad, Dr. Warren Mastoon, for teaching me about offering kindness and a generous spirit to the world; my sister, Lisa Mastoon, for her unconditional love, tireless editing, and for telling it like it is; my brother in-law, Eric Pritchard, for his counsel and support; and my nephew, Samuel Elliot Pritchard, for his laugh that lights up the world.

I thank my friends for loving and listening to me and every last detail of this project. Pat Alvarez, Gina Angelone, Revital Arieli, Inbar Barkama, Rakefet Barkama, Toni Herbine-Blank, Jennifer Block, Dennis Caraher, Stephen Cope, Aruni Futuronsky, Janice Gitterman, Catherine and Mitch Hinard, Russell Kaye, Sarah Lesser, Connell McGrath, Tulsi Murray, Paula O'Hara, Hally Pancer, Lee Rubinstein, and David Waitz. Their presence in my life supports, renews, and sustains me.

Finally, I want to thank the people at William Morrow who took this book into their hearts and offered their impeccable talents: Doris Cooper, my editor, whose commitment and care enrich the pages of this book. I am grateful for Doris's patience and for taking thousands of my calls. I want to thank Fritz Metsch for his exquisite design. Special thanks to Tom Nau for his commitment to excellence in the reproduction of these photographs. Susan Pearson had the vision to see the impact that this book could have on the lives of young people; and Will Schwalbe championed and believed in this book from the beginning.

My deepest gratitude for all of the help, seen and unseen, that made this book possible.

The Shared Heart Initiatives is a nonprofit organization the mission of which is to promote awareness, understanding, and acceptance of the diversity of sexual orientations, particularly of lesbian, gay, and bisexual youth. The Shared Heart Initiatives endeavors to educate about these issues through healing art and educational resource materials in order to foster the development of safe and supportive environments in which all young people can learn and thrive. An exhibition of the images presented in this book is touring high schools, colleges, and workplaces. If you would like more information, please write to: The Shared Heart Initiatives, P.O. Box 562, Brookline, Massachusetts 02146.

◐

Designed by Fritz Metsch
Produced by Tom Nau

Composed in Walbaum MT, Linotype Astrology Pi A
and Copperplate Gothic 33 BC by
Westchester Book Composition,
7 Finance Drive, Danbury, Connecticut

Duotone separations by
Jaguar Advanced Graphics'
39 Wyandanch Avenue, Wyandanch, New York

Printed and bound by
Kinsgsport Press,
Press & Roller Street, Kingsport, Tennessee